D0966873

Scooter Mania!

Scooter Mania!

Willy and Max Schlesinger*

* (and their dad)

Safe, Fun Tricks and Cool Tips for Today's Hottest Ride

St. Martin's Griffin
New York

www.stmartins.com

Interior photos by John B. Carnett

Book design by Margo Mooney, pink design, inc.

ISBN 0-312-27832-2

First Edition: December 2000

10 9 8 7 6 5 4 3 2 1

The authors want to thank **Basic Wheels**—
www.basicwheels.com—the best scooter shop in New York
City and probably the world.

Important! Read This Now!

A lot of the pictures in this book were taken in the street. What you don't see in the pictures are the adults who were at either end of the street stopping cars from coming down. Scootering in the street is much more dangerous than biking in the street. You shouldn't do it! And especially, you would never try to perform tricks in the street! Ever! Most of the tricks included in this book can be done on sidewalks or driveways. The street is no place for a kid on a scooter. **Readers are urged to wear helmets and safety gear whenever they ride and to think safety first.**

Contents

Introduction: How It All Began   1

1.   Scooter Components: Parts and Stuff   7

2.   Which Scooter Is Right for You?   27

3.   The Best Places to Ride (Safely)   37

4.   Scooter Reviews   51

5.   Taking Care of Your Scooter   61

6.   How and Where to Buy Your Next Scooter   79

7.   Accessories   85

8.   Tricks and Activities   91

    Glossary   109

Scooter Mania!

Introduction

How It All Began

*I*t sounds strange to say that scooters are back. If you're a kid, you probably don't remember when scooters were here the first time. That's because when scooters were around the first time it was when your grandparents or even great-grandparents were kids.

The first scooters weren't bought in stores—they were all handmade by kids. This is the way the first scooters were made. Kids then liked to roller-skate. That's what they called it back then, roller skating, not in-line skating. This was back before most kids even had those skates that were pretty much leather boots—like an ice skate—with wheels stuck on the bottom. These early skates were metal frames with wheels on the bottom that fit over your regular shoes and attached with leather straps. You could adjust the size of the skates to fit your shoe. These skates were made of two pieces—front and back—with a bolt in the middle that you tightened so that they wouldn't slide apart and they'd fit your shoe. Kids used what was called a skate key to tighten this bolt; a lot of times they'd wear the key around their necks on a piece of string.

These old-fashioned skates were a lot different from today's in-line skates. They had four wheels—two in front and two in back—and were made out of really clunky metal. The ball bearings inside the wheels were really cheap.

Kids back then couldn't go as fast on their skates as a kid on in-line skates can today. Because the wheels weren't made great and because sidewalks and streets were more bumpy back then, kids on metal skates couldn't get up any speed. It was more like walking on wheels than skating on ice.

Plus, there was almost no glide back then. Today you can get up to a good speed and glide or coast for fifty or sixty feet. On metal skates you were lucky to coast along for five or ten feet.

Back then, riding around on skates was a pain. You could feel the vibrations all the way up your legs and in your knees. Plus, the wheels would get dinged up and the bearings would crack.

What this meant is that the skates broke . . . a lot. So many kids had only one skate, because the other one was broken. They had to think of some way to use the good skate. What a lot of kids did was to take the good skate apart by unscrewing the middle bolt. This produced two halves, each having two wheels.

Kids would then attach half a skate to either end of a length of wood. The best wood was usually a two-by-four, because it's about the same width as a foot and fit the skate halves well. At this point, the device looked kinda like a really skinny skateboard.

The next thing kids did was get a wooden box from the local fruit and vegetable stand. They would then nail the box to the front of the length of wood. The box in the front made the piece of wood with the roller skate attached to it look something like a car. Okay, maybe not the kind of cars you are used to, but remember, cars were still box-shaped back then.

However, and more important, the box gave the kids something to hold on to when they pushed their homemade scooters. The box was like a steering wheel.

By today's standards, these scooters were really lame. There was a lot—A LOT—wrong with them. For one thing, they were dangerous. Kids would push forward on the box, the nails would come out of the two-by-four deck, and the kids would go crashing over the box. And they were really hard, if not impossible, to steer. That's because most of the time the skate wheels were just nailed into the wood. You couldn't turn them very well! Plus, you couldn't go half a block without getting a splinter from the box. And finally, the wheels would come out of the wood as the nails were pulled out by wear and tear.

These early scooters were death traps! But hey, what else could they do with only one roller skate and a piece of wood?

Next came actual scooters made in factories; these worked pretty well in comparison to the homemade scooters. They had pretty big rubber wheels—four or five inches around—and the decks were made of pressed metal. They also had a steering column and handlebars. The larger, rubber wheels gave a smoother ride than the roller-skate wheels, and you could actually steer around corners. Also, the decks were wide enough to fit both feet while you coasted. Some of them even had rear brakes a lot like the brakes on the Razor-type scooters.

There was only one problem. These scooters were mostly designed for girls or really little kids. The simple fact is, boys liked bikes better.

Scooters Come Back

If you're reading this book, you already know that scooters are back in style. And we're not talking about your grandpa's scooter, either. The scooters today are slick, sleek, and hip. They aren't made out of old two-by-fours and busted skates, either. They're made out of new high-tech materials and have precision bearings and polyurethane wheels. And they're designed for a smooth, safe ride.

However, they do have a few things in common with the old-fashioned scooters. You still power them the same way, by pushing them along with one foot. And you still steer them with a column on the front.

And if you think about it, scooters have a lot in common with in-line skates, which are pretty much roller skates. We'll discuss the specifics later in the book, but the truth of the matter is, in-line skate wheels and bearings and all the rest are really what make scooters better than ever. So there's still a connection between roller skates—uh, blades—and scooters.

Adults and Scooters

Kids aren't the only ones riding scooters today. Grown-ups are riding them, too.

There are a lot of theories about why adults like the new scooters. Some adults say that riding scooters makes them feel young again . . . yeah, right. Hey, coming home at night and doing two hours of homework, struggling through long division and fractions without a calculator might make them feel young again, too. But you don't see many adults doing that, do you?

The *real* reason adults like scooters is because scooters are cool. Even the most basic scooters are well-designed, sleek, and easy to ride. Yes, even an adult can hop on and ride it right away. Compared to skateboards and in-line skates, scooters are a piece of cake. Remember, most grown-ups can't ride skateboards and aren't very good at in-line skating. If you've ever watched an adult try out a skateboard or in-line skates, then you know it can be pretty hysterical. However, with scooters, adults can just hop on and zip along the first time. This isn't quite as funny, but at least they're not hurting themselves.

Scooter Tip #1

THE SECRET TO SAFE TURNING IS BALANCE. BE SURE THAT YOUR FEET ARE PROPERLY POSITIONED ON THE DECK WHEN TURNING. IT IS POSSIBLE TO TURN WHEN PUSHING, BUT ONLY IF THE FOOT YOU ARE USING TO PUSH IS THE ONE OPPOSITE THE DIRECTION YOU ARE TURNING IN. THAT MEANS, IF YOU ARE TURNING RIGHT, YOU PUSH WITH YOUR LEFT FOOT. IF YOU ARE TURNING LEFT, YOU PUSH WITH YOUR RIGHT FOOT. PUSHING WITH THE LEFT FOOT AND TURNING LEFT OR PUSHING WITH THE RIGHT FOOT AND TURNING RIGHT WILL LEAVE YOU UNBALANCED.

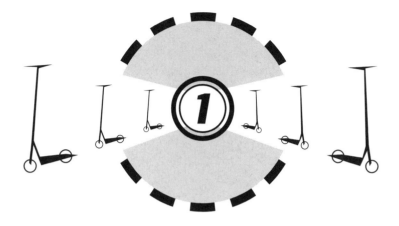

Scooter Components: Parts and Stuff

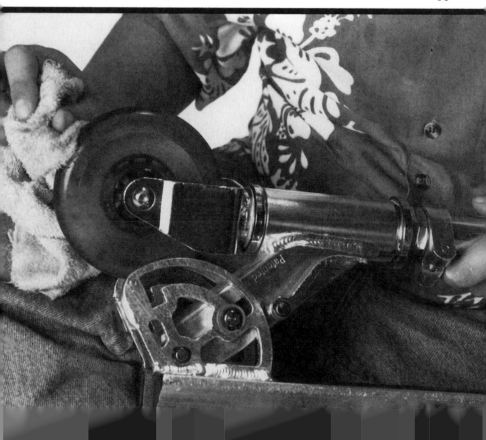

First off, all scooters have several parts in common. For instance, all scooters have wheels. All scooters have decks—the platform you stand on while scooting. And all scooters have steering mechanisms.

Take away any one of those things—wheels, deck, or steering column—and you don't have a scooter. It's as simple as that.

History of the Wheel

Now, let's take a tour of the scooter from the ground up, starting with the wheels.

Today's scooter wheels owe a big debt to skateboaders. Yeah, it's hard to admit, but true. What happened is this. The first skateboards—called sidewalk surfers—were invented back in the late 1950s. These early boards were basically pieces of wood wider than a two-by-four with skate wheels mounted on the bottom. They were kind of like an old-fashioned scooter, only without the box nailed to the front.

Surfers liked these boards, even though they were noisy and didn't work very well. The boards provided the surfers with something to ride when the waves in the ocean weren't big enough. Surfers could use their balance and surfing skills to ride around streets.

These first skateboards had the standard metal wheels from roller skates. Early skateboarders learned what kids with scooters had known for a long time—the metal wheels were less than great. First off, they had no traction. Secondly, the metal did nothing to cushion the shocks from the bumps and lumps in the street or sidewalk. (Think of riding in a car with metal tires.) And last, the bearings were inferior.

Next came wheels of a hardened clay that had much better traction. They came from the roller-skating industry. Clay wheels were popular for the indoor rinks, because they didn't ding up the floor like metal wheels, weren't as noisy, and gave the skaters a smoother ride. But there were problems with the clay wheels, too. For one thing, they were too fast . . . way too fast. People got hurt on skateboards (this was before safety gear was widely used). And for another thing, clay wheels were almost as hard as the metal ones, so you could feel every bump and lump in the road.

Then something cool happened: plastics. Back in the early 1970s, a guy named Frank Nasworthy discovered urethane (that's pronounced: Your-a-thane) wheels. Urethane is a tough plastic, but it has a lot of cool features that make it ideal for street riding. Nasworthy saw this immediately and began making wheels for skateboards.

Frank Nasworthy didn't actually discover urethane. It had been around for a long time. It was invented in Germany at the Bayer company, the same company that makes aspirin.

Polyurethane has some characteristics that make it ideal for scooters and skateboards. First, it has really good traction. The added traction means speed, but it also means control. When you turn your scooter or skateboard, it will hold on to the ground and not slide around. Also, because polyurethane wheels are softer than metal or clay ones, the ride is much smoother. And polyurethane is sturdy, so it lasts a long time. It is pretty resistant to heat and light, so it won't fade, melt, or permanently bend out of shape from use. And finally, because it's plastic, you can mold it to almost any shape you want.

The polyurethane wheels really took off when it came to skateboarding and roller skating and, of course, in-line skates. Then scooters . . .

So, why is all this stuff important? First of all, because you're learning something. Second, because there are manufacturers and stores who sell proven products. These stores can include larger sporting goods stores that have in-line skate and skateboard supplies or specialty stores that have only in-line skate and skateboard supplies. If you have an in-line skate, skateboard, or scooter shop near you, then we suggest you go there for wheels and other supplies even if you didn't buy your scooter there. The reason for this is simple—the guys in the skate shops usually know their stuff. They know the differences in wheels and bearings and all the rest of it. Plus, if you run into any problems, then they can probably help you out. They're the experts.

Wheels

Okay, we're discussing just the Razor and scooters like the Razor for now. Wheels have several different characteristics to consider.

Yay for the Mesopotamians!

*I*f it hadn't been for the Mesopotamians who were hanging around at about 3500 B.C., then we wouldn't have scooters. That's because they probably invented the first wheels. Before that, people would just drag stuff around. Try a scooter without wheels some time—it's no fun. If you thought wheels were invented in caveman times, then you've been watching too many cartoons.

SIZE

First the sizes. The standard Razor wheel is 100 millimeters in diameter. The word *diameter* means the size of the wheel in cross section. Basically it means how big the circle is from the bottom through the center to the top. Millimeter is abbreviated mm. Most Razors can fit a wheel up to 110 mm, except for the one that has a shock absorber system. That particular model will fit only a 100 mm wheel.

Why would you want a larger wheel? Well, it is slightly faster than a smaller wheel. You might also be able to find different hardnesses and colors in the larger wheel that are not available in the standard wheel.

There is hardly any advantage to the larger 110 mm wheel against the 100 mm wheel.

PROFILE

When you look at a wheel from the front you can see how it is shaped and that it is either thick or thin. This shape is called the profile. Some wheels are more blunt and offer a more stable ride. Other wheels are skinny at the bottom and top and offer a less stable ride, but more maneuverability. Naturally, the thicker wheels last longer than the skinny wheels.

But if you ride your scooter where there are a lot of bumpy sidewalks with cracks, then the skinny wheels will not only wear out much faster but may cause you to crash more often.

HARDNESS

In addition to different sizes, wheels come in different hardnesses, too.

When you look at a wheel or its package, you'll see what is called a durometer rating. A durometer is simply an instrument that measures the hardness of something.

SCOOTER COMPONENTS: PARTS AND STUFF

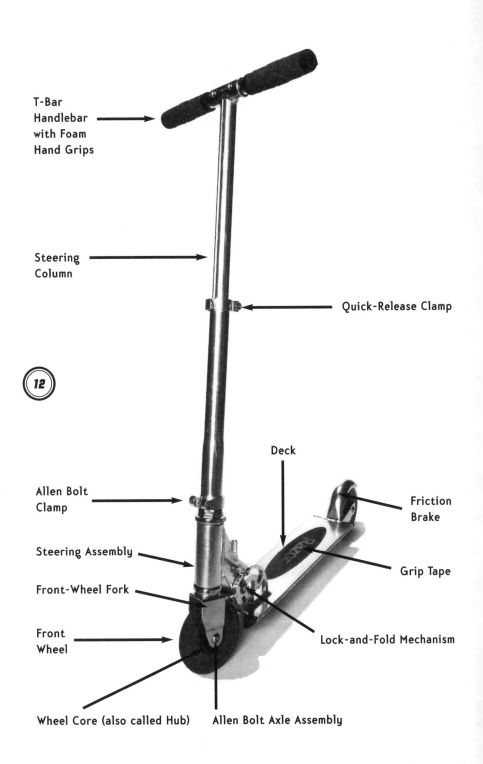

T-Bar Handlebar with Foam Hand Grips

Steering Column

Quick-Release Clamp

12

Deck

Allen Bolt Clamp

Friction Brake

Steering Assembly

Grip Tape

Front-Wheel Fork

Front Wheel

Lock-and-Fold Mechanism

Wheel Core (also called Hub)   Allen Bolt Axle Assembly

The out-of-the-box Razor-type scooters have wheels with a hardness rating of about 85A or so. The ratings go all the way up to 100A, so an 85A is a medium-hard wheel. A lot of serious in-line skaters go for a hardness rating in the 90s at most.

Now remember, the harder the wheel, the faster it goes. So what's the big deal? Why not just get the hardest wheel you can? Well, for one thing, the harder the wheel, the bumpier the ride is going to be. Believe it, with a really hard wheel you'll feel every single pebble as you ride along.

So if you're not into speed, why not go with a softer wheel? Unfortunately, the really soft wheels won't last as long. They get chewed up by cracks in the sidewalk and get chunks taken out of them. They also bend out of shape more quickly if you ride a lot.

A larger wheel with the same hardness rating as a smaller wheel will have more bounce and cushion than the smaller wheel. You can prove this to yourself by dropping a smaller wheel and a larger wheel on the ground and seeing which one bounces higher.

Choose your wheels carefully. A lot of kids just pick their wheels for color and don't pay attention to the ratings, but those ratings are important. If you just want to ride along smoothly with friends, then go for an 80. If you want to speed around and even do a few tricks, then go for an 85 or higher.

HUBS

The hub, which is also called the core, is the center of the wheel that holds the bearings in place. The hub is made of a stiff material that also keeps the wheel straight. It is particularly important for softer wheels because they bend more easily and thus need more support at the center.

If you need new wheels, always buy wheels with cores or hubs. Some very cheap wheels do not have hubs. There are two kinds of hubs: *open core* means you can see the spokes and supports, and *closed core* means that the spokes and supports don't show. With more spokes you have a lighter wheel but a harder ride. However, wheels with more spokes will not bend as much.

Also, many in-line skaters believe that open core wheels keep the wheels from becoming too hot and softening the urethane.

Bearings

Next to wheels, the bearings are the most important part of the scooter. You may not realize this, because you never see the bearings, but they're there. Bearings are fitted into the center hole part of the wheel core. Most wheeled toys have bearings. Bearings make the wheel turn easily and smoothly.

Bearings are round metal cases with metal balls (ball bearings!) in them. When the axle is put through the bearing case it is touching only the tops of the metal balls, which spin. This means that very little surface area of the ball bearings is touching metal, but the axle is still being moved smoothly around by the tiny balls. Cool, huh? Very cool, because if the axle or other metal was spinning in a metal sleeve and touching metal all around, then the axle and whatever held it would not only spin more slowly, but would get really hot because of the friction.

Another reason why bearings spin so freely and create little friction and heat is that they are oiled. A thin layer of oil on the tops of the balls keeps the metal sleeve that goes around the axle from directly touching them. Instead, the sleeve is riding on a tiny layer of oil.

If you can't picture what a bearing looks like, then do this: Draw a circle on a piece of paper. Now, inside that circle, draw another circle made up of seven or eight little circles, like a necklace. That's a very basic bearing.

Now, if you want to see how bearings actually work, find a cheap bead necklace—please, don't use your mom's pearls!—and make a small loop with the beads big enough to fit your finger through, but snug. Now move your finger around inside the loop. It should move pretty easily. That's because the beads are turning with your finger. Try the same thing with a piece of rope and you'll see that the rope will not only turn with your finger, but your finger may even start to get warm. It gets warm because of friction. That's what bearings do—they reduce friction!

There are two different types of bearing cases: enclosed and open. In the enclosed shield type of bearing case, the case is sealed and you can't get at the little ball bearings. In the removable shield type of bearing case, you can open the case to clean and lubricate the ball bearings.

Most high-end—expensive—bearings come with a removable shield to let you clean the bearings. However, enclosed shields work fine, too. When it comes to scooters, either type is fine. It just depends on how technical you want to get.

Bearings, like wheels, are rated, but they are rated with what is called an ABEC number. ABEC stands for the Annular Bearing Engineers Committee.

And who is in charge of the committee? That's easy: the Anti-Friction Bearing Manufacturers Association. Now, aren't you glad you asked?

Bearings are rated from 1 to 9, softest to hardest. A lot of the scooters out there today have ABEC ratings of 5, which is fine for most people. There are also some bearings that have ratings higher than 9; these are made out of super-space-age ceramics.

Before you get crazy and start begging your parents for the super-fast ceramic bearings, let's be calm and think about it. The ABEC ratings were created not for scooters, but for factories. Many expensive and high-powered machines use bearings to run smoothly. The guys who make bearings—the Anti-Friction Bearing Manufacturers Association (remember, them? A cool bunch of guys!)—developed ABEC bearing ratings so that the companies who made the machines would use the right kind of bearing in their machines. ABEC measures how precisely the bearings are made, whether they are being used in super-high-speed turbine engines or in scooters.

ABEC is what is called an industry standard rating. This means that whatever company makes the bearings, they are measured and rated in the same way. Another industry standard, for instance, would be shoe sizes. There may be small differences between a size 6 1/2 shoe from one company and one from another company, but all size 6 1/2 shoes are pretty much the same size. This makes shopping for shoes a lot easier. The same is true for bearings. An ABEC 5 is going to be pretty much the same, no matter who makes it.

However, when in-line skaters and skateboarders started paying attention to bearings, they noticed the ratings. "Hey, ABEC 9 has to be better than ABEC 5!" they said. Whether this is true or not, at least it gave them something to talk about. Because, let's face it, a huge machine working in a factory needs more precision than a kid doing Ollies in the schoolyard.

Types of Scooters

There are two basic types of scooters out there now: the ones that have the in-line type wheels and a narrow deck and those that have a larger wheel and a wider deck.

Why do the scooters with larger wheels have a wider deck? The answer is easy. Because the wheels are larger, they have a longer glide or coasting distance. That means your feet are spending much more time on the deck resting than on the ground pushing.

Which type of scooter you decide to buy depends on a lot of things, like your budget and where you plan to ride. If you buy more scooter than you need, then you are wasting money. If you buy less scooter than you need, then you won't have a good time.

Scooter Tip #2

WHEN RIDING IN GROUPS, BE SURE TO LEAVE ENOUGH ROOM BETWEEN YOUR FRIENDS IN FRONT, TO THE SIDE, AND BEHIND YOU. IT IS MUCH HARDER TO RIDE IN GROUPS WITH SCOOTERS THAN IT IS WITH BIKES BECAUSE SCOOTERS GO FAST, THEN SLOW, THEN FAST AGAIN, AND EVERYONE DOES NOT MOVE AT THE SAME SPEED.

Big Wheels on Scooters

Good Because They Are:

◎ ARE FASTER
◎ OFTEN HAVE A BETTER GRIP
◎ ALMOST ALWAYS PRODUCE A SMOOTHER RIDE
◎ ALWAYS HAVE A LONGER GLIDING RANGE
◎ DON'T GET CAUGHT IN CRACKS AS EASILY

Small Wheels on Scooters

Good Because They Are:

◎ MADE IN MORE COLORS
◎ LESS BULKY, MEANING THE SCOOTER FOLDS UP SMALLER AND WEIGHS LESS
◎ MORE EASILY REPLACED
◎ EASIER TO CLEAN
◎ VERY MANEUVERABLE AND ALLOW FOR SHARP TURNING

Why Larger Wheels Are Faster

W hy do larger wheels go faster? Here's an explanation that starts with an experiment. A bike wheel and a scooter wheel are good for this experiment because the middle metal part (axle) around which the wheel turns is about the same size.

Take a piece of tape and tape a straight line from the axle (axis) to the outer edge (perimeter) of the wheel. The line the tape makes is called the radius.

Now, line both wheels up so the tape lines are both straight down pointing to the ground. Mark the ground below both lines with a piece of chalk, basically just continuing your tape line on the ground. That's your starting line.

Then slowly roll the bike wheel forward until the tape line has gone once around, back to where the tape meets the ground again. Make another chalk mark and connect the marks. Do the same thing with the scooter wheel; line the tape up with the ground; slowly roll the scooter forward until the line meets with the ground again; and mark the spot with chalk and connect the marks. The bike wheel traveled much farther, right?

Now, if the bike wheel and the scooter wheel both go around, say, ten times in five seconds, what do we know? We know from our experiment that the bike wheel is going farther, but it is also going faster because the bike wheel covered a greater distance in the same amount of time— that's called speed. Speed is just measuring any distance traveled by using time to do the measuring.

In physics, speed is called velocity (v), and it is measured by the distance (d) traveled in a given or set amount of time (t). So velocity equals distance divided by time: velocity = distance ÷ time. Or $v = d/t$.

You're doing physics. Linear velocity, or how far you go in a given amount of time, is usually expressed in cars, bikes, and scooters as miles per hour (mph). Like 5 or 60 mph, sound familiar? Let's do just a little more physics so we fully understand our wheel speed or velocity. Every time a wheel goes around once, it's called a revolution. When measuring the speed of a spinning object (wheel), people talk about revolutions per minute, or rpm's. Again, sound familiar? How many times a spinning object goes around is called angular velocity. Angular velocity is different than linear because a spinning object goes around its own middle (axis or axle). This basically means you can turn your bike or scooter upside down and spin the wheel forever and it won't go anywhere. However, if you are measuring the speed of a spinning object that is in contact with something else—say, the ground—you can measure the linear velocity in relation to the angular velocity or the relationship between miles per hour (mph) and revolutions per minute (rpm). In simple terms: how fast the car wheels (angular velocity) spin determines how fast the car goes (linear velocity). Easy, right?

Now, linear velocity (v) equals angular velocity, or times a wheel goes around (w), multiplied by the radius (r) of the object, or the length of that piece of tape that travels from middle of the wheel to the outer edge. Or in scientific terms, $v = wr$.

To get down to the conclusion: For every turn (revolution) of a little wheel, you travel a set distance. And for every turn of the bigger wheel, you are covering more distance than the little wheel. Going back to the experiment, the little wheel has to turn more times to cover the same amount of distance.

NOTE: TECHNICAL INFORMATION AND FORMULA PROVIDED BY THE AMERICAN SOCIETY OF MECHANICAL ENGINEERS (ASME).

Forks

Almost all scooters have front forks. The fork is the U-shaped unit that holds the wheel and attaches to the steering column. Scooters that are styled like the Razor also have a rear fork as well. In almost all cases, the forks extend up to the steering column and another set of ball bearings, just like a bike. In some scooters, the fork is attached to a shock absorber.

It is absolutely essential that the fork be sturdy. In the Razor, for instance, it's made out of stainless steel. If you are shopping for a scooter and the fork seems flimsy, then stay away from it. Not only won't the scooter last, but it could be dangerous to steer after it wears out.

Trucks

Some scooters don't have a rear fork, but rather a truck, like a skateboard. And a couple of makes of scooters have front trucks as well.

Trucks support the weight of the rider, give enough flexibility to steer, and hold the axles (and wheels) in place.

Most trucks contain a base plate, the metal plate that holds the truck to the deck. These base plates are usually held in place by four screws or bolts. You should check them every once in a while to make sure they are secure.

The kingpin on the truck is the wide bolt that holds the truck itself to the base plate. The kingpin can be loosened to provide more flexibility in turns, but it should never be really loose. Also, there are usually rubber bushings included in the truck where it connects to the base plate. If you take the truck off, make absolutely sure you include these bushings when you put it back. They not only make for a smoother ride but keep the truck from wearing out too quickly.

The last part of the truck is the hanger, which basically holds the axles. Even if the truck is made out of aluminum—as many of them are—the axles should be steel.

Brakes

Every scooter should have a brake. Brakes come in two basic designs. The most popular is a foot brake, which is located at the rear. It's a very simple design that you work by putting your foot down and pushing the metal against the rear wheel.

The second type of brake is the hand brake or cable brake, which is similar to those you see on bikes. Both kinds of brakes work, though the foot-brake may take a little getting used to. Also, the hand brake gives a little better control.

There are a couple of reasons why your scooter should have a braking system. First, a brake will save your shoes. If you are always slowing your scooter down with your feet, it won't be long before you wear out your shoes. Plus, braking with your feet can throw you off balance.

The second reason is safety. A good braking system allows you to slow down on hills.

Some kids say that the brake isn't important because skateboards don't have brakes. True, skateboards don't have brakes, but skateboards also have four wheels, and most scooters only have two wheels. And because scooters have only two wheels, the rider needs more control, particularly when it comes to speed.

Also, skateboards have trucks that you can turn by leaning left or right. Scooters, like bikes, turn by handlebars, so you need to slow down a lot of times to turn, just as you do on your bike.

Decks and Frames

The platform you stand on is called a deck. The deck is the largest and most noticeable part of a scooter. There are many different styles of decks. Some are designed just to look cool and some are designed with a specific purpose in mind.

The deck and frame can be attached permanently as one piece or in two separate pieces. In some scooters, like the Razor, the deck and the frame are pretty much one piece. In other scooters, like some of the wide-bodied ones, the deck can be removed from the frame.

There are thin decks, wide decks, long decks, and short decks. There are also wood decks and metal decks. There are even high-tech plastic decks.

To begin with, frames should be sturdy. The steering column should be securely attached, and if you have one of those scooters that fold down, the mechanism should also be securely attached. This can be difficult to tell, but if the frame and steering column aren't secure, then the scooter is dangerous.

Also, kids want to know what the difference is between wide decks and thin decks. The answer is easy.

Thin decks, like the one on the Razor, are good for scooting around the block and maneuvering. If you travel long distances, you might want a wider deck. Also, if you want to coast more and push less, you might want a wider deck. Think about it: If one of your feet is not on the deck a lot of the time, pushing or waiting to push, then you really don't need the room. However, if you glide for long distances, then you might want a larger deck that easily holds both your feet. Also, if you are going fast on downhill runs, the larger deck provides better balance.

The major advantages of the smaller decks are easy to see. They fold up smaller and are generally lighter and maneuver, turn, and jump better.

The two main things you should look for in a deck are weight and durability. That's why many decks today are made of aluminum. Not only is aluminum lightweight, but it's also sturdy.

Decks also come in different materials. Probably the most common material used is aluminum. Some people don't like aluminum decks because they don't flex or bend.

A deck that flexes or bends, like a skateboard deck, provides a smoother ride. Such decks are usually made of plywood or layers of wood and fiberglass.

There are other materials that are also light and durable, though expensive, such as carbon fiber. And some scooter manufacturers offer models with swappable decks. That means the decks can be removed from the frame and changed or upgraded. So if you get bored with the wood deck, then you can change it for an aluminum deck. However, most of these scooters are expensive.

Steering Columns and Handlebars

Most steering columns today are adjustable for height. If you're a kid who is still growing, then this is a great idea. It also enables you to fold the scooter up when you're not using it.

There are several different locking and folding mechanisms available today. When you shop for a scooter, make sure the column locks firmly into place. Also make sure that the handlebars fit snugly.

If you're shopping for a scooter and the steering column doesn't lock firmly into place, don't buy it. The wiggle in the column will only get worse over time.

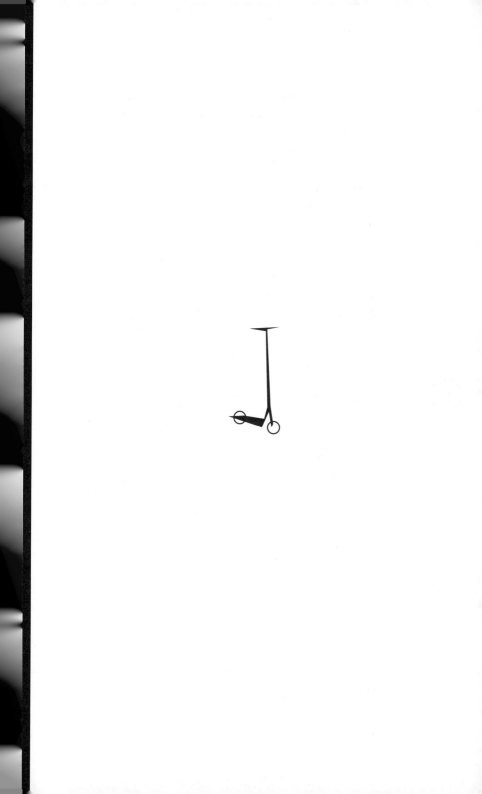

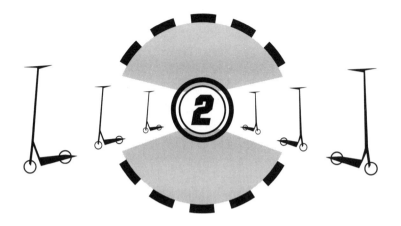

Which Scooter Is Right for You?

*N*o doubt about it, there are a ton of different scooters out there. The scooter you choose depends on a lot of stuff.

Price

Buying a scooter is a lot like buying a car. First you have to decide how much you can spend. You have to establish a budget. The more stuff you get, the more expensive the scooter is going to be. Some scooters are very basic and some are very fancy. Sure, you might want that sleek new carbon-fiber deck and front brakes. But can you afford them?

On the other side, if a scooter is too cheap, then watch out. When the Razor became popular, many manufacturers started making scooters. Some of these are fine, but some are shoddy. Check out the locking mechanisms, the wheels, and all the other parts. If the manufacturer used plastic or obviously inferior materials on the stress points, such as locking mechanisms or forks, then stay away. These scooters won't last as long as well-built scooters, and they can be dangerous.

Style

Kids often want scooters that look like their friends' scooters. There's nothing wrong with that, and it may be a good thing, since your friends have already tested them.

If you plan on buying a scooter like your friends' scooters, ask if you can test-drive their scooters first. This way you can tell if it's the right scooter for you. Don't go crazy and ask to ride it for a week. You should be able to tell if you are comfortable on the scooter after a short test drive.

Also, if you are going to buy one of the really expensive scooters, then ask the person in the store if you can test-drive it. If the salesperson won't let you at least try it out for size, braking, and glide, then go to another store. After all, you wouldn't buy a car without taking it for a spin.

Decks, Brakes, and Wheels

Some of the stuff you may think is for show might really serve a purpose. For instance, decks come in a lot of different styles. Some of the wider decks look cool, but they are also great for long cruises down hills. So if you are going to cruise a lot, then you may want a wider deck.

The same thing is true for bike-style hand brakes. Hand brakes are cool, but they also provide better control. This is good to remember if you plan to travel down lots of hills pretty fast. Hand brakes are also good to have if you are going to be scooting someplace where there are twists and turns.

Wheels are something else you should know about when buying a scooter. Smaller wheels, like on the Razor, are very maneuverable. However, you can also crash more easily on smaller wheels.

If you are going to scoot in a schoolyard, park, or parking lot that is pretty smooth, then smaller wheels are great. Bike paths are also pretty smooth and shouldn't give you any problems. However, some sidewalks have a lot of big cracks in them. Sometimes tree roots break up the path and sometimes the squares are just worn and old. If the cracks in the sidewalk are wider than the wheel or stick up, then you may have problems.

The rule is: The smaller the wheel, the more problems you will have with sidewalk cracks. You may already know this from in-line skating. Cracks you can zoom over without a problem on your bike can cause real problems on a scooter if your wheel gets caught in them.

If you live someplace where there are a lot of cracks and uneven sidewalks, then you may want to think about getting a scooter with larger wheels, which won't get stuck in the sidewalks as easily. However, larger-wheeled scooters are much faster. Speed isn't a problem on flat surfaces, but on hills it can be *very* dangerous.

Steering Columns and Handlebars

Steering columns and handlebars help you in three important ways. First, they are how you steer the scooter. Second, they help you balance on the scooter. And third, when you push back with your foot, you are also pushing against the handlebars and steering column.

If you're a kid, then you should probably go with adjustable handlebars. Most of the scooters available for purchase have adjustable handlebars, so this shouldn't be a problem. The reason adjustable handlebars are better is because kids come in all different sizes. Face it, a kid who is six or seven likes to ride on a scooter as much as a kid who is ten or twelve years old. Yet the six- or seven-year-old is a lot shorter than the older kid.

Making sure that the steering column and handlebars are set at the right height is important for your safety and comfort. Getting the right height adjustment often involves testing to see what feels and works best. You shouldn't be hunched over the handlebars or reaching up to grab them. They should be at a comfortable level, near your center of gravity, so that your arms are slightly bent.

Safety Gear

Safety gear is really important, particularly if you're going to be scooting fast or are doing stunts.

Safety gear for kids should always include a helmet. Wrist, elbow, and knee guards should be used, too, especially if you are going fast or doing tricks. These things will help you avoid what skateboarders call road rash, those painful scrapes you get when you fall on asphalt or cement.

Scooters have some advantages over skateboards. It's easier to step off a moving scooter than it is to step off a moving skateboard. Stepping off the scooter before the crash can help you a lot. Kids tend not to go very fast on scooters when they are just scooting around. Also, skateboarders tend to do more tricks than scooter kids. But you can get going pretty fast on a scooter.

If you started out with in-line skates or a skateboard, you may already have some of the safety gear you need, such as a helmet and wrist guards and elbow pads. However, some wrist guards are too tight and don't allow your hand to move freely to steer. This can be a problem. A good alternative is a pair of well-padded BMX bike gloves. Many kids are using the BMX-style bike glove with the fingers cut out as scooter gloves. These gloves don't give as much protection as rigid wrist guards, but they are padded and offer pretty good protection. Also, ankle pads can help soften those smacks to the ankle that happen when the scooter deck swings back toward you when you step off to avoid a crack or bump in the road.

Helmets Are Always a Good Idea

GUESS WHAT? A LOT OF KIDS (AND ADULTS, TOO) ARE HURT EVERY YEAR RIDING BIKES, SKATEBOARDING, AND IN-LINE SKATING. SOME THEM ARE HURT A LOT WORSE THAN THEY SHOULD HAVE BEEN, ALL BECAUSE THEY DIDN'T WEAR A HELMET.

AND GUESS WHAT ELSE? IF YOU RIDE A SCOOTER—OR A BIKE OR SKATEBOARD—YOU ARE GOING TO FALL. OH, YEAH, YOU'RE TOO GOOD TO FALL, RIGHT? BUT IF YOU HIT A ROCK OR A HOLE OR SOMEONE ELSE HITS YOU, THEN YOU'RE GOING TO FALL. SO WHY NOT WEAR A HELMET AND PROTECT YOURSELF? THERE ARE SOME EXCELLENT SKATEBOARDING AND BIKING HELMETS OUT THERE. CHECK THEM OUT. BUY ONE. AND WEAR IT!

Safety Checklist

1. If you have a collapsible scooter, check all locks, locking mechanisms, and releases to make sure they are secure before you get on the deck.

2. Never ride more than one person on a scooter.

3. Be considerate of those walking. Never try to swerve in and out of foot traffic or race where there are pedestrians.

4. Don't hitch rides. Never attach your scooter to or grab onto any motorized vehicles or even bikes.

5. Be familiar with the terrain. Uneven surfaces are the major reason scooter riders fall.

6. Don't try complicated tricks, even if you have done the same tricks on a skateboard.

7. Wear light or brightly colored clothing when riding at dusk or dawn. Bike safety lights and reflective clothing are also a good idea. Scootering at night is dangerous, even if you know the terrain. A small unseen rock or stick can send you flying.

8. Wear shoes with rubber or nonskid soles. Shoes that aren't firmly fastened to your feet, such as flip-flops or clogs, are not good scooter shoes. Skateboard sneakers, such as Vans, are great for scootering. They have flat rubber soles that really grip the deck and the sidewalk as you push off. Plus, they are rough and tough enough to take abuse, so they'll last a long time.

9. Large helmets, portable stereos, or anything else that obstructs your view or hearing are not a good idea. You can't get out of the way of danger if you can't hear or see it coming.

10. Follow the same traffic laws you do on your skateboard or in-line skates.

11. Always keep both hands on the handlebars. One-handed or no-handed riding reduces your stability. Remember, because the front steering column is on bearings to help you turn easily, you can't ride a scooter like a skateboard! This is very basic, but kids forget it sometimes. You need to control steering at all times.

Riding Safely

You have all the safety gear. You've checked out your scooter for any possible malfunctions. Now what?

A SCOOTER IS NOT A SKATEBOARD

You should know what you can and can't do on a scooter. Because a scooter looks like a skateboard, a lot of kids think that it can do the same things that a skateboard can. No, a scooter is different from a skateboard. Skateboard wheels are not only much wider, but there are four of them. Not only that, but the four wheels are attached to a flexible truck that helps the boarders balance even when they are on uneven inclines or jumping curbs.

Most scooters have two skinny wheels that are mounted on a rigid axle and have very little flexibility. Also, scooters often have little flex in the deck. A skateboard's flex helps you to control it for jumps and other tricks. Without that flex, tricks are difficult and dangerous.

What Dares Really Mean: A Real-Life Translation

*K*ids are always daring other kids to do something really stupid. With scooters, a dare might mean going down a steep hill or trying a dangerous trick. Dares can put you in real danger. Smart kids don't take stupid or dangerous dares. Some kids, though, don't know what dares really mean. So here's a translation.

He says: "I dare you to . . . "

He means: "I'm too smart to try it, but you do it, because I think you're stupid."

He says: "I double-dare you."

He means: "It might be cool to see you get hurt."

He says: "What a wimp! C'mon, just do it!"

He means: "It'll be cool if you get hurt and bleed. Maybe even break a leg or something."

He says: "My big brother's friend did it."

He means: "If an ambulance or the police show up, then I'm running away."

Scooter Tip #3

BECAUSE MANY SCOOTERS DO NOT HAVE SHOCK ABSORBERS, JUMPING CURBS AND BUMPING OVER SMALL OBSTACLES ADDS WEAR TO YOUR WHEELS AND BEARINGS. WHENEVER POSSIBLE, AVOID JUMPS AND BUMPS.

A SCOOTER IS NOT THE SAME AS IN-LINE SKATES

Just because a scooter employs the same wheels as in-line skates doesn't mean that you can do the same kind of tricks. True, in-line skates are mounted on firm axles, but the cushioning and flexibility comes from the in-line skater's knees and legs. In-line skaters can also move their feet in combinations that give them balance and control.

Many of the tricks that you see either in-line skaters or skateboarders perform are impossible on a scooter. They shouldn't even be attempted because they are so dangerous.

Riding on a scooter is fun and there are tricks you can do on it. But you should never mistake a scooter for either in-line skates or a skateboard.

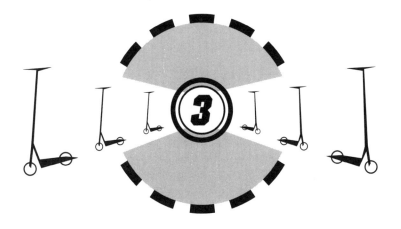

3

The Best Places to Ride (Safely)

*T*he very best places to ride are smooth, well-maintained paths free of cars. These would include parks, playgrounds, schoolyards, and sidewalks.

Of course, if there are no cars, then there are probably bikes, skateboards, in-line skates, and all the other people-powered traffic. This is true for bike paths and parks. In playgrounds, you have little kids and adults to watch out for.

You should obey all the rules of the road when scooting in these places. That means going slower in playgrounds and not blocking the traffic on bike paths. Scooters can be a problem on bike paths, because they go fast when you first push off, then slow down, then go fast again and slow down again. This pace can cause a problem for bike riders, who need to judge speed to pass you. If you're riding on a bike path with a lot of other people-powered traffic, stay to the right, where bike and in-line riders can pass you more easily. If you are scooting with friends, ride single file on bike paths.

Kids on scooters also go kind of zigzaggy when they are not paying attention. So remember to move straight ahead when scooting on a bike path.

Also, some bike paths are for bikes only. That means no skateboards, no skaters, and *no scooters.* If there's a sign that says "Bikes Only" or shows a skateboard or a skate in a circle with a line through it, that means no scooters. This may not be fair, but it happens. Breaking this rule and going in a bikes-only path means that you're not only breaking the rule but doing something dangerous. People on bikes going fast won't expect to encounter a kid on a scooter, and there could be an accident.

Rain, Rain

Because a lot of scooters have urethane wheels without treads, they may not have good traction on wet surfaces. Even a puddle can make for a slick ride when you go

ALWAYS USE THE CORRECT TOOLS WHEN WORKING ON YOUR SCOOTER. ALLEN WRENCHES ARE A MUST-HAVE FOR CHANGING THE WHEELS ON MANY DIFFERENT STYLES OF SCOOTERS. USING THE WRONG TOOLS CAN HURT THE BOLTS OR NUTS AND MAKE THEM MORE DIFFICULT TO REMOVE.

through it. So if you are riding on wet ground, you may not have as much control over your scooter. Think about it. Tires on cars, trucks, and bikes have treads, the pattern on the tire that helps it grip the road. Many scooters have smooth wheels with little gripping power. Plus, the scooter wheels are much harder than inflatable tires. All of this means that they don't hold the road firmly. Especially when it's wet.

Know What Is at the Bottom of a Hill

Riding downhill can be a lot of fun. You get to glide all the way down without pushing off. It's always a good idea to know what's at the bottom of a hill. A hill that bottoms out in the middle of a four-lane highway is not a good scooter hill. Even a hill that ends in a turn may not be a good scooter hill if you can't make the turn safely.

When you ride downhill, don't be afraid to use your brake to slow the speed. If you feel that you're going too fast, then you probably are. It's always better to be safer rather than faster.

Mud, Ice, and Sand

Avoid all three. Mud, ice, and sand are dangerous to scoot on or through and can get into your bearings and mess them up. Other stuff that can make you fall and get into your bearings are gravel, sawdust, and the little chunks from wood chips. You should stay away from all this stuff as much as possible.

Feet ahead: Keep your feet pointing ahead. And when you are gliding along without pushing off, keep one foot close to the brake.

Indoor Scooting

If you are going to scoot in an open indoor space, such as a gym, make sure your wheels are free of tar and dirt because they will leave stains on the floor. Some colored wheels leave marks on a floor. If you are going to be scooting on a carpeted floor, be aware that some carpets may be slick. Also, linoleum, wood, and tile surfaces can be slippery. A good general rule to follow is that harder wheels are better for indoor use and softer wheels are good for outdoor use.

Riding Styles

If you are used to riding a skateboard, then you probably started riding your scooter with both feet facing sideways. This is okay. It gives you a solid position on the deck and good balance. However, you have to twist your body sideways to hold the handlebars and your push-offs can be a little awkward. On long glides, such a position is not bad, but if you're going to be pushing and gliding and pushing and gliding for any distance, you may get a backache.

A better position is for one foot to be on the deck facing straight ahead. That means your big toe is pointing right at the steering column. This moves your body to the forward position, eliminating that half turn.

However, some people walk with their toes pointing either outward or inward. That's the way they balance best and feel most comfortable. If you are one of those people, then it's perfectly fine to point your toe and foot a little to the side.

Another common mistake kids make is to snug up right to the steering column. This can throw the scooter's balance off. The foot that you don't push off with should be a little way back on the deck from the steering column. That way, when your other foot comes back up from pushing off, you are better balanced in the middle of the scooter.

Go, Go, Sir Isaac Newton!

Sir Isaac Newton was one of the greatest scientists of all time. And he would have loved scooters, except he lived around three hundred years ago.

He would probably have loved scooters, because he would have understood how they worked—scientifically speaking.

He thought up three laws, which are called Newton's laws of motion. Will they help you become a better scooter rider? Probably not. If you know them, will you be smarter? Yep.

Newton's first law of motion says that an object that is at rest—not moving—will remain at rest until some force makes it move. A good demonstration of this is to put your scooter down and step back. The scooter won't move. Wait an hour and watch it. The scooter won't move unless somebody or something moves it.

But wait, there's more! The second part of the law says that an object that is moving will continue to move in a straight line unless some force stops it or causes it to change direction.

Can this be true? Will something keep going and going without any extra help? If this was true, then you could push your scooter once and go around the world. That would be true, except there are a lot of forces to stop it—for instance, friction from the wheels turning. Bearings reduce the friction but don't eliminate it. Also, the wheels run on the ground, which creates friction.

So if you eliminate all friction, will your scooter go faster? Yes, but you won't like it, because the friction of the front wheel on the ground is what lets you steer. If you've ever ice-skated and had a hard time stopping, then you know what a lot less friction feels like.

Newton's second law is pretty easy to understand. It says, basically, that the speed of a moving object is related to the force that made it move. Push on your scooter hard—using a lot of force—and it will go fast. Push on it lightly and it will go slow.

The second part of this law says that the mass (weight) of the object being moved is related to how much force it takes to move it. This is simple—the bigger something is, the more force it takes to move it. That's why you sometimes see little kids zooming along on scooters and adults can't go fast. Little kids don't have to push as hard as adults to reach the same speed because little kids are lighter.

Newton's third law of motion says that for every force, there is an equal and opposite force. You use this law every time you get on a scooter. You are pushing back with one foot to make the scooter go forward. Simple.

Will knowing these three laws help make you a better scooter rider? Probably not, but you learned something!

Let's Go Already!

It's always better that the scooter falls, and not you. Remember, the scooter can't feel scratches and road rash! If you feel like you're losing your balance and are going to fall, then get off the scooter. If you can hold on to the handlebars safely, then fine. However, if it feels that the scooter is going to pull you down, then just let it go.

This technique works great when you hit a crack in the sidewalk and you are not going too fast. If you are going fast, then use the brake first to slow down. It's always important to feel completely in control of the scooter. If you are going really fast and don't feel 100 percent in control, then slow down with the brake.

Holding and Pushing

The basic push or kick is as easy as walking. First, you should have a firm overhand grip on the handlebars. Second, plant one foot securely on the deck. And then push off with your other foot. Most kids that are right-handed (which means they throw and catch with their right hand) prefer to use their left foot for powering their scooter. This is because their right foot seems to give them better balance. Kids that are left-handed tend to use their right foot for power. Whichever way you feel most comfortable and balanced is the right way.

The Need for Speed

The first push should be a long one, if you have enough room. This first glide will give you a moment to rearrange your hands or foot for the best balance.

The push is like running. The longer the stride, the farther the glide. With a good firm push, most of your foot should come down on the ground.

But scooting is not exactly like running. It takes a second for the scooter to gain speed from the push and then a few seconds to start losing speed. The best way to go fast is to push once, then wait a second and then push again, wait a second and then push again, and again and again. In this way, the scooter gets all the speed it can from the first push and then more speed is added by the second, third, fourth, and fifth push. This is pretty normal, and the second you should wait will automatically be spent bringing your foot back into position after the last push.

You are adding energy (speed) when the scooter is going its fastest. Knowing this can help you if you're having trouble keeping up with other kids. It will also keep you from wasting effort. If you aren't going as fast as you think you should or get more tired than the other kids, then you may be adding energy (pushing) when the scooter isn't moving at its fastest. You may be pushing when the scooter is either slowing down or speeding up from the last push. To gain speed you should do long, steady pushes.

However, long, steady pushes can be difficult to keep doing when you are going fast. Depending on how fast you are going, shorter pushes will do the same to maintain or gain speed.

Scooter Tip #5

NEVER RIDE TWO ON A SCOOTER. NOT ONLY IS THIS DANGEROUS, BUT IT CAN AFFECT YOUR BALANCE AND CAUSE YOU TO FALL. ALSO, IT ADDS STRAIN ON EVERY PART OF THE SCOOTER.

Comfy Cruising

Kids like to cruise in different ways. Some kids like to push off, then glide for as long as they can before pushing off again. There is nothing wrong with that. It's a perfectly fine way of scooting. Fast and then slow can be a lot of fun.

However, if you want to maintain a steady speed, the trick is to time your pushes to the scooter's speed. When you scoot for speed, you add energy (push) when the scooter is reaching the fastest part of the glide. When you are cruising along, you want to add energy (push) when the scooter is slowing down. If you add the same amount of energy at the same point in the glide, then you will go at a steady speed.

That is not as difficult as it sounds. Like the explanation for adding speed, it mostly just puts into words what you may already be doing, but it doesn't hurt to understand what is happening. The secret is steady pushes at the same place in the glide. If you can establish a rhythm of medium-long pushes, then you should be able to glide along at a steady speed.

Hand Positioning

You should keep a firm grip on the handlebars. This is the same grip you use when riding a bike. It's important that you keep a two-handed grip on the handlebars. Unlike a bike, which you can ride one-handed or even no-handed, a

Use both hands: Always keep both hands on the handlebars with the palms down, just like riding a bike.

Wrong: With the under-hand grip you can't steer as well and your balance is not as good.

Really wrong: With a one-handed grip your balance and steering are really bad. Using only one hand to steer is asking for an accident.

scooter requires even better balance. Plus, your front wheel requires more steering.

Some kids make the mistake of thinking that riding a scooter is the same as riding a skateboard with a steering column and handlebars. This is not true. A skateboard has four wheels, not two like a scooter. Those two extra wheels make all the difference when it comes to staying balanced.

For the best possible balance, position your hands palms down, an equal distance apart on the handlebars. This is easy, because the grips are located an equal distance apart. Moving one hand closer to the center steering column will throw your balance off.

Another possible hand position is the underhand grip, holding the handlebars with your wrists and palms up. This is not a great cruising or speed position. However, it is worth knowing because it can help you when doing tricks. If you want to pop a wheelie, but aren't strong enough to pull up the front end, you might try this. But be careful. Remember, your balance will not be as good with the underhand grip.

Know About Balance . . .

Balance is the most important thing when it comes to scootering, bike riding, skateboarding, and in-line skating. If it's so important, then why don't we ever think about it?

Try this experiment. Get on your scooter and try to balance. Don't go anywhere. Don't push. Just keep the scooter perfectly still and try to balance upright. Not too easy, is it? The same thing is true for bikes. They are easier to balance when they are moving.

There's a simple explanation for this. It's called precession. Precession is a force generated by circular spinning objects, like wheels, for example. Precession is the force that keeps your bike from toppling over while you're riding.

Precession is a natural phenomenon that is generated because the center (axis) of a spinning object naturally aligns itself straight up and down, whether vertical, like a bike wheel, or horizontal, like a CD in a CD player.

If you have ever had a toy gyroscope, then you have seen precession in action. In fact, you have seen it in action with a toy top. Precession is the reason a top stays upright when it's spinning.

The faster an object spins, the stronger the precessional force it generates. Unfortunately, with scooters and bikes, there are much stronger forces at work, like your body weight, so scooters and bikes will tip over.

Here's an experiment you can do with an adult. Get an old bike wheel on its axle and hold it between two hands, then have someone else spin it very quickly. Once it gets going fast, try to tilt it left or right. You will notice that it feels like it's pushing back to stay straight. That's precession!

Accidents: They Happen

What can anyone say? Accidents happen. If you have a scooter, skateboard, bike, or in-line skates, then you are going to fall. You may not fall today or tomorrow, but eventually you will—and you may get hurt.

Most accidents in scootering can be avoided by simply stepping off the scooter. That's the beauty of them. If the thing is falling, you can just let go and let it fall without you. Sometimes you can even keep a hold on the handlebar and save the scooter, too.

Here are a few tips for avoiding accidents:

Don't race on sidewalks. Most sidewalks are too narrow to race on and have too many cracks to go fast, safely. If you are going to race, then race in an open area where you can maintain a safe distance from your opponent or opponents.

Maintain control at all times. If it feels like you are going too fast, then you *are* going too fast. Slow down.

Avoid little kids and pets. Parks and playgrounds are packed with people, pets, and little kids. Never race or show off tricks in an area where there are pets or little kids around. Go slower whenever there are other people nearby, particularly little kids.

Walk your scooter over curbs and across streets. There are two very good reasons for this. Hopping curbs adds wear and tear to your wheels, bearings, and frame. Skateboards regularly hop curbs, but they have more flex and better shock-absorbing properties built into the trucks and wheels. Also, it's dangerous. A car may turn the corner without the driver seeing you. Hopping a scooter off the curb, even when the light is green, doesn't give you enough time to check traffic and look both ways before crossing the street.

Ouch! This could have been a bad fall, if he hadn't been wearing his safety gear. Always, always, always, gear up for scooter riding.

A Short History of the Band-Aid

*B*and-Aids were invented by a man named Earl Dickson. He worked at Johnson & Johnson, the company that makes Band-Aids. Back in 1920, Mrs. Dickson hurt herself a lot in the kitchen. And back then, people cut up pieces of gauze and tape and wrapped that around even little cuts.

For Mrs. Dickson, cutting up gauze and tape was difficult when she had a cut finger. So Mr. Dickson took some adhesive tape and gauze and put the gauze on the tape in little sections, so that his wife could bandage herself up whenever she had a cut. These first Band-Aids were just little squares of gauze on short lengths of tape.

When Mr. Dickson told his boss about the solution to his wife's problem, he thought it was a good idea, too. Soon the company was making Band-Aids and has been making them ever since.

Scooter Reviews

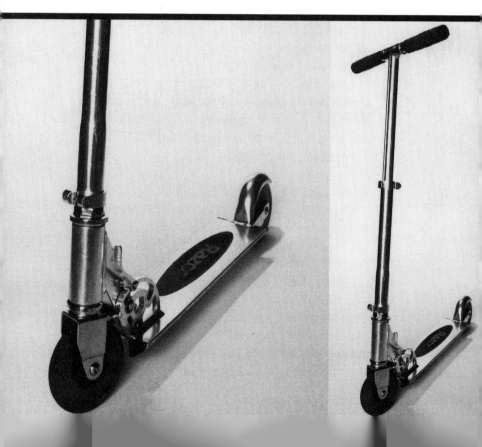

*T*he information kids want to know about a scooter is if it is cool-looking and if their parents will buy it for them. Kids also care about some of the features, such as brakes and decks, wheels and steering. So that's the kind of information you will find below. There aren't a lot of numbers and technical stuff. If you need more information, go on the Internet and find it on the manufacturer's Web page or visit your local scooter shop.

The scooters listed below are the most popular ones, and they will give you an idea of what is available.

Remember, before you buy any scooter, shop around and compare features and prices. Ask the salespeople in the store if you can take it for a test drive for a few feet or at least stand on it to check the balance and fit.

Some scooters out there are really expensive. These scooters are mostly made for adults who like to scoot. A lot of these scooters are very well designed and made. But before you buy one or ask your parents to buy you one, ask yourself: Is it worth it?

You should also be wary of super-cheap scooters. If a scooter is really cheap, it may not last as long as a name brand. Plus, it could be dangerous to ride after a while. As a scooter rider, you depend on your wheels, axles, and steering column to hold up.

Xootr Scooters (www.xootr.com)

The Xootr (pronounced *zooter*) is probably the best scooter in the world. These scooters are made by a company called Nova Cruz and have been called the Rolls-Royce of scooters.

These scooters are sturdy, well-made, fun to ride, and expensive. They're a lot more expensive than the standard Razor scooter, but you can see the quality. The big question is: Do you want to spend that much money for a scooter?

If the answer is yes, then there are three main types of Xootr scooters from which to choose.

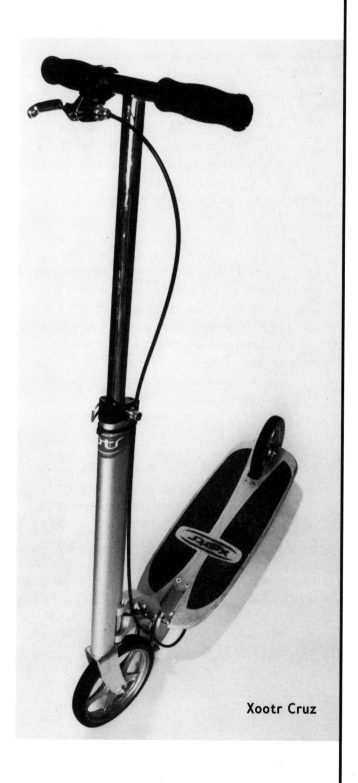

Xootr Cruz

THE XOOTR CRUZ

This scooter has a sturdy wood deck and 7.1-inch wheels that are specially made of polyurethane with aluminum cores. The frame is made from quality aluminum and is quite stylish. The brake is a bike-style hand brake system that offers really good stopping control.

The deck is also much wider than a Razor—almost 8 inches!—so it's a good scooter for cruising.

THE XOOTR STREET

The Xootr Street is also a high-quality scooter, but instead of a wood deck, it comes with a really cool, very light aluminum deck. The Street has the same 7.1-inch wheels as the Cruz; these wheels are designed for speed, with a very fast, smooth-gliding polyurethane outside and aluminum rims. Again, there's a bike-style hand brake for the rear wheel.

Again, the deck is very wide, almost 8 inches, and great for cruising around.

Both the Cruz and Street weigh about 10 pounds.

THE XOOTR COMP

This is a top-of-the-line scooter. The deck is made out of very cool, sturdy, and extremely lightweight carbon fiber. Plus, the Comp includes all the features on the other two scooters, including the wide deck and bike-style brakes. It also has the very fast Xootr wheels.

All three of these scooters are great. They are all light-weight and all fold up pretty small. And all three of them are good for cruising and racing. However, price can be a big drawback. All three of them are more expensive than most bikes made for kids.

Also, Xootr scooters may be too big and fast for smaller kids. Smaller kids should have a scooter that is right for their weight and height.

K2 Kickboard

The K2 is a weird-looking scooter. The second you look at it, you'll notice the differences. For one thing, it doesn't have a regular set of handlebars. It has a kind of joystick steering. This would seem like it would be really difficult to steer, except that the wheels don't turn like those on a regular scooter. The two 100 mm front wheels (that's right, two!) are mounted on a skateboard truck, so you steer it like a skateboard and scooter combination. Believe it or not, this works really well. You get a lot of control, but it takes some getting used to if you've been riding a standard scooter. Riding the K2 is a little like riding a combination snowboard, skateboard, and scooter. The deck also has a great bouncey feel to it, similar to a skateboard. This is good for doing tricks and it absorbs a lot of the rough spots in the road. The K2 is also very light—about 6 pounds—and like other scooters, it folds up.

The one drawback is that the K2, like the Xootr models, is not cheap and may not be right for smaller kids. It costs a lot more than the Razor, though it's made by the same company that makes the Razor.

KnowPed

The KnowPed scooters are made by the same company that makes Go-Ped motorized scooters. They basically took the motor off these models. That's a good thing, because the motorized scooters were made to last. The KnowPed has a steel frame, which means it'll last, but it's a little heavier than aluminum. It also has thick solid rubber tires. These are great for not getting caught in sidewalk cracks.

This model also has a bike-style hand brake and back brakes. And there's an extra wide deck.

The KnowPed is definitely built to last. It's also built for long cruises rather than fast scooting. This is the scooter that your biggest adult relative can step on and you won't worry about the thing snapping in two.

California Chariot

This is kind of like a tricycle scooter. It has three wheels, so balance isn't a problem, and two decks, so if you have humongous feet, you have someplace to put them.

The Chariot is definitely not the kind of scooter you can fold up and carry around with you. The Chariot also has a bike-style hand brake, so it's easy to stop.

The best thing about the Chariot is that it comes in two styles: the regular standard style Chariot and the California Chariot Skooch. The Skooch is made for little kids, so they can enjoy scootering, too.

The Razor (www.razor.com)

What is there to say? It's small. It's aluminum. It's everybody's favorite scooter. It folds up so small that you can almost put it in your backpack. And it isn't outrageously expensive.

The Razor has a narrow deck and collapsible handlebars. The rear brake is foot-operated. And it's an excellent all-around scooter.

There are a few drawbacks to the Razor and scooters like it. For one thing, it doesn't do well on uneven or bumpy sidewalks. The little wheels get caught easily. Second, it isn't good over long distances. The narrow deck can be a bit cramped if you are an older kid or adult with big feet.

However, the Razor and other scooters of the same style are still the best all-around scooter for kids.

One thing about the Razor is the name. This has caused confusion around kids. Some of the scooters have the name Razor and others the name JD Razor on them. Which is the official Razor? The answer is—they both are! After importing the Razor for a couple of months, the company changed the name to the JD Razor. It's the same scooter and the same company, just a slightly different name.

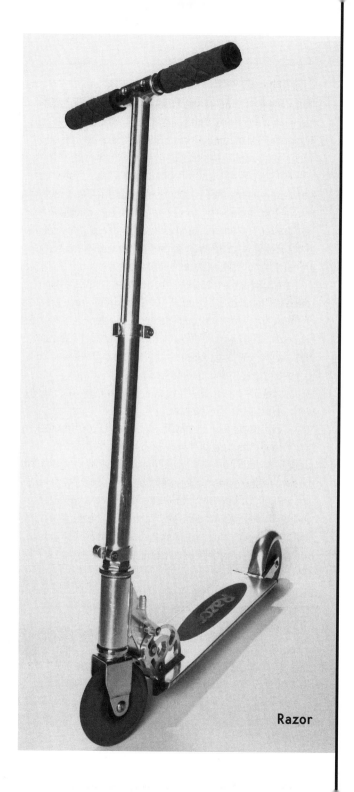

Razor

Other Brands

These are just a few of the scooters out there. Naturally, there are a lot more. And some of the other scooters are great. Whichever scooter you choose, there are a few things you should check before taking it out of the store:

Brake. Every scooter—no matter what!—should have a braking system. This is absolutely essential. Don't let anyone tell you otherwise. It doesn't matter whether it's a rear contact brake, a bike-style hand brake, or any number of other styles—as long as it's easy to operate and works properly. A scooter without a brake is a dangerous scooter.

Adjustable steering column. If the steering column is too low or too high, then you won't have the kind of control you need to scoot safely. A scooter's steering column should adjust to your size for a comfortable ride. Plus, the locking mechanism should hold the column firmly in place. If a steering column has wiggle in it after it is locked, then it's probably no good. That wiggle will only get worse as you use the scooter.

Grip tape on deck. Think about it: you are putting pressure on the foot that you keep on the deck of the scooter. If your foot slips around on the deck, then you will have an unsteady and uncomfortable ride, and a dangerous one as well. (If your grip tape wears out or comes off, then replace it. You can get new grip tape from the manufacturer or a skateboard shop. Many skateboard shops sell fancy grip tape with a variety of patterns and images on it.)

Warning:

SOME VERY CHEAP SCOOTERS OUT THERE ARE SOLD WITHOUT GRIP TAPE. THE SECTION OF BOARD THAT SHOULD BE GRIP-TAPED IS JUST PAINTED BLACK. THESE SCOOTERS CAN BE DANGEROUS. AVOID THEM. HOWEVER, IF YOU ALREADY HAVE ONE, THEN BUY SOME GRIP TAPE AND APPLY IT.

Grippy handlebars. You should have some kind of handlebar grips. Almost every single scooter sold today has them, but to cut costs, the manufacturers of some of the less expensive scooters are putting on inexpensive ones. The handlebar should provide you with a firm grip. (If your handlebar grips wear out, you can replace them with either bike grips or a new set from the manufacturer.)

Quality parts. Let's face it—there are some really cheap and really bad scooters out there. Before you buy a scooter, ask your friends which make and models they bought and if they were happy with them. Find out if any of the parts on their scooters needed replacing. And before you buy a scooter, inspect it. Look for cracks in the plastic parts, like the clamp that holds the steering column into place. Jiggle all the parts to make sure they fit tight with little or no wiggle. Turn it upside down and spin the wheels to make sure they spin evenly and smoothly.

About Those Motorized Scooters . . .

A lot of kids are interested in those very cool motorized scooters. Yes, they are cool. They're also dangerous. Some of them go up to 20 miles an hour or more. That doesn't sound very fast, but it is. And when you think about how you are balanced on just two small wheels, then it's very fast. One expert we talked to said that anyone who rides one of the electric- or gas-powered scooters should be at least old enough to drive a car.

In a lot of areas, they're not legal. What that means is, just by riding it on a quiet street, you're breaking the law.

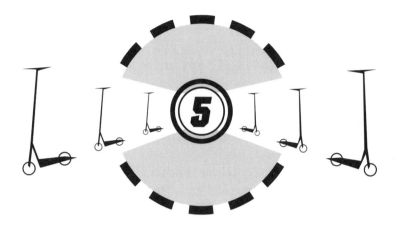

5

Taking Care of Your Scooter

Basic Repairs

You can do a lot to keep your scooter running smoothly for years, including cleaning and changing different parts of your scooter. However, some things you should *not* try to fix. For example, if a welded joint from your scooter breaks, you should not try to fix it yourself the best you can. Take the scooter back to the store where you purchased it or call the manufacturer.

A more common problem is the locking parts. If you have a folding scooter and the piece that locks the scooter into the riding position breaks, take it back to the shop and have them install a replacement part. The same is true for the lock or clamp that adjusts the height of the steering column.

Remember, the right parts installed correctly means safer scootering.

Take care of your scooter and it will take care of you. Your scooter is just like your bike. If you neglect it and throw it around, it won't last very long. Scooters today are made to last, but even quality construction and parts won't last very long if you don't take care of them.

Each part of your scooter needs a different type of care and cleaning. Much of the maintenance is similar to the care you take of your bike, but some of the stuff you should do is different. Here's a step-by-step guide to basic scooter maintenance.

USE ONLY THE CORRECT TOOLS FOR THE JOB. BY USING THE WRONG TOOLS, YOU NOT ONLY MAKE THE JOB MORE DIFFICULT BUT ALSO RUN THE RISK OF DAMAGING PARTS. MOST SCOOTERS TODAY ARE DESIGNED SO THAT THEY CAN BE REPAIRED AND MAINTAINED WITH SIMPLE AND EASILY OBTAINABLE TOOLS. ALSO, NO SCOOTER REPAIR JOB REQUIRES A HAMMER, A CHAIN SAW, OR A MACHETE.

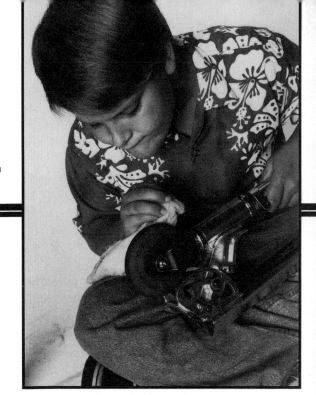

CLEANING THE WHEELS

After you scoot, your wheels will probably be dirty. This is
a bigger problem than dirty bike wheels. For one thing, a
lot of kids bring their scooters inside the house, so you
can get dirt on the floor. Also, the dirt and grime and all
the rest of that stuff can get into the bearings, and that's
bad—really bad. So you have to keep the wheels clean.

You can use a mild spray cleanser—the mildest you can
find—or a damp cloth or paper towel on the wheels to get
off most of the dirt and gunk. The worst thing you'll find on
your wheels is tar. Tar is a lot harder to clean. To get tar or
oil off, use a mild citrus-based cleaner. Don't use nail polish
remover or turpentine or any strong stain removers. Some
skateboard and in-line skate shops sell special cleaners for
wheels. Check them out. If you don't have a skate or skateboard shop near you, then check out the automotive section of your local chain store.

Whee
whee
espe
ride
insid
gunk
whee
the

Scooter Tip #6

SOME HOUSEHOLD CLEANSERS ARE VERY DANGEROUS. A
WITH AN ADULT BEFORE USING THEM TO CLEAN YOUR SC
CITRUS-BASED CLEANERS ARE STRONG AND SHOULD BE
WATER BEFORE USING.

Wheels

THE CHECKUP

Get into the habit of checking your wheels before you
scoot around. Even if you don't feel anything unusual o
weird about the way they ride, it's always a good idea t
check, just in case.

The best way to check your wheels is to sit down
with the scooter turned upside down in your lap. Turn
each wheel slowly and check for dings, nicks, and chunk
removed. Such damage can happen when you get the
wheels caught in sidewalk cracks.

While you are spinning the wheel slowly, check for w
If the wheel looks crooked on one side, then it's worn dow
and should be replaced. A wheel that is worn down enoug
can throw your balance off. Also, when a wheel becomes t
thin, it catches in the sidewalk cracks more easily.

If your wheels seem to be wearing out on one side a
not the other, then you can try doing what in-line skater;
do, which is called flipping. This simply means changing t
left and right sides of your wheel, so that the left side is
now on the right and the right is on the left. This can add
extra miles to your wheels.

Next, wiggle the wheel. Make sure it isn't loose.
If the wheel is loose, then tighten it up or have a parent
tighten it with an Allen wrench.

NOTE: IF YOU HAVE RIDDEN YOUR SCOOTER AROUND AT ALL, YOU WILL NOTICE THAT THE VERY BOTTOMS WILL BE A MILKY WHITE AND NOT AS CLEAR AS THE MIDDLE OF THE WHEEL. THIS IS NORMAL.

REPLACING WHEELS

On most scooters, you can easily replace the wheels. Many manufacturers sell replacement wheels for their scooters. You can order them through your local skate, skateboard, or bike shop. You can also order them on-line at the manufacturer's Web site.

In most cases, wheels are very easy to change. Most kids get into problems when they order wheels. There are a few things you have to know before ordering:

Model. It always helps to have the model name or number of your scooter. If you have a Razor, then you have to know if it is the kind with a shock absorber or without a shock absorber. The front shock makes a difference when it comes to front wheel size.

Size. Check the size of the wheel you buy to make sure it will fit on your scooter. And if you are changing just one wheel, make sure it is the same size as the old wheel. Some wheels have the size listed on the side and some do not. If you don't know the size, then bring the wheel you are replacing to the store. If you are buying wheels on-line, check your owner's manual for standard sizes and specs.

With or without bearings. Make sure you know if the wheel you are buying comes with or without bearings. You can always move your old bearings into a new wheel, but it is much easier to use replacement wheels that have bearings already in them.

NOTE: IT'S ALWAYS BEST TO REPLACE BOTH WHEELS. IF ONE WHEEL IS BENT OR CHIPPED AND HAS TO BE REPLACED AND YOUR OTHER WHEEL IS JUST WORN DOWN BUT STILL GOOD, YOU SHOULD STILL REPLACE BOTH WHEELS. THAT'S BECAUSE THE WORN WHEEL THAT STILL WORKS MIGHT BE A LOT SMALLER THAN THE NEW WHEEL.

Bearings

THE CHECKUP

Spin your wheels again. Do they spin funny? Maybe you hear a little grinding sound. That could be dirt in your bearings. Sand from a sandbox, gravel from a playground, and other stuff can get in there and cause that noise. And, most serious, it could be a worn-out pair of bearings.

Even if your bearings are just dirty and not worn out, this is still bad news. Dirty bearings can turn into worn-out bearings pretty quickly. That's because the dirt or sand or whatever else is in there will cause more friction and wear down the bearings.

Next, spin one wheel medium fast and check to see how long it spins. Then spin the other wheel at the same speed. They should spin about the same amount of time. If one spins a lot longer than the other, then you may need to clean and lubricate your bearings.

BASIC OILING AND CLEANING

A lot of skateboard and in-line shops sell fancy lubricants and oils for bearings. These work fine, but good old household oil—the kind you'd use for your bike chain, not the kind you use for cooking—works pretty good, too. The best types of oil come in a container with a little needle-type applicator. This applicator lets you put drops of the oil right where the bearings are located. It's a pretty good invention and works well for scooters.

However, remember not to put too little or too much oil on your bearings. This is very important! Too much oil will attract dirt and other gunk that will ruin the bearings over time. With too little oil, the bearings will wear out faster. Six drops of oil is plenty. If you use any more, most of it will leak out, anyway.

Read the service manual and check with the authorized dealer before attempting any maintenance work. If you cannot find the manual or dealer, then try contacting the company directly.

If you aren't mechanically inclined, a lot of skateboard and in-line stores will clean and oil your bearings for a small charge. Also, different scooters have different ways of removing the bearings, so it's also always a good idea to check with an expert on your particular model.

Some bearings come shielded in an enclosed case and others come in a case with a removable front. Those who are into serious skateboarding and in-line skating like the idea of opening the case to get at the little ball bearings in order to clean them one by one. This isn't really necessary on a scooter.

Even closed bearings should be oiled and cleaned every once in a while. A light oiling and cleaning around the outside will extend their life.

NOTE: THERE ARE LOTS OF DIFFERENT TYPES OF LUBRICANTS FOR BEARINGS. JUST BECAUSE AN OIL OR OTHER LUBRICANT IS MORE EXPENSIVE DOESN'T MEAN THAT IT IS BETTER. THE KIND OF HOUSEHOLD OIL YOU USE FOR YOUR BIKE CHAIN IS FINE. OTHER, MORE EXPENSIVE LUBRICANTS INCLUDE TEFLON, AND THESE ARE GOOD, TOO. THE MAIN THING IS TO OIL BEARINGS REGULARLY—EVERY COUPLE OF MONTHS—AND NOT TO OVER-OIL OR UNDER-OIL.

Cleaning and lubricating your bearings is a good job to do with an adult. That's because it can be kind of tricky. If you have in-line skates and have taken care of those bearings, then this job is pretty much the same.

The right (and left) tools: Two Allen wrenches are best for removing most wheels. You need to use them at the same time to work best. Be positive you have the right size because once the bolts are ruined they are difficult to remove.

Careful work: Once you get the wheel out of the scooter, put both screws someplace safe, like in a bottle cap. So you don't lose them. Then inside the wheel you'll see a spacer ring that moves. With a thin instrument, like a little screwdriver, move it aside and push the bearing at the other end out. Push carefully at the side of the bearing. If you push too hard you can dent the bearing.

Clean and oil: If you have the kind of bearings that can't be taken apart, then you can clean and oil carefully from the outside. Remember too much cleaner is bad for the oil inside the bearings. Just clean as best you can with a small rag and a little cleaner.

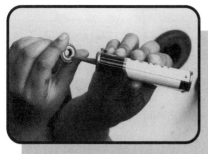

Oils well that ends well: A few drops of oil at the center seal should do it. Remember: Too much oil attracts gunk that can slow down your bearings. Wipe extra oil from the outside of bearing with a non-oily piece of rag.

1. Take the wheel off the fork. You will probably need an Allen wrench for this.

2. Pop the bearing out of the center of the wheel. This sounds easy, but it can be difficult. You might need a bearing-removal tool. An in-line skate shop should have this special tool. Depending on the type of bearings you have, you might have to remove the C-ring from the bearing case before you try using the bearing-removal tool.

3. Once you have the bearings out and the case opened (if it is the kind that opens), then place the bearings on a rag or paper towel and soak them with a good cleaner such as paint thinner or degreaser. Do this outside or in a well-ventilated area.

    Wait awhile before moving on to the next step. You want the bearings to be dry before oiling them.

4. After all the dirt and grime and old lubricants are removed, then re-oil them. Remember to use just the right amount of oil. If you use too much, you will attract a lot of dirt. If you use too little oil, the bearings will wear out quickly from friction. If there is a spacer between your bearings, remember to clean and lightly oil it. The spacer is a short metal tube between two bearing cases that keeps the bearings from being pushed too far into the wheel.

For bearings with removable guards:
Pin pointy: Use a pin to remove the bearing's C-ring. Just put the pointy end of the pin in the opening of the C-ring and gently lift.

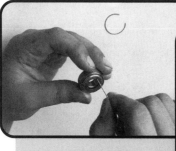

Guard off: Once the C-ring is off, remove the guard by lifting it with the pin. Inside you'll see the guts of the bearing. If it's filled with gunk, then clean it out carefully; otherwise, just add a few drops of oil and put the bearing back together.

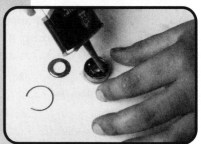

5. Remove whatever extra oil there is on the case with a clean paper towel or rag.

6. After you re-oil, hold the bearings between two fingers and spin. This will help work the oil around inside. Also, check for that pesky grinding sound. If it is still grinding, then you may need new bearings.

7. Use a damp cloth to clean the center hole in the wheel.

8. Reinsert the bearing case into the wheel.

REMEMBER, THIS CAN BE A VERY TRICKY PROCESS. DIFFERENT SCOOTERS HAVE DIFFERENT KINDS OF BEARINGS. TO BE ABSOLUTELY SAFE, HAVE EITHER AN ADULT WHO KNOWS WHAT HE OR SHE IS DOING HELP YOU OR TAKE IT TO AN EXPERT AT THE SCOOTER DEALER OR IN-LINE SHOP.

When Good Bearings Go Bad

Your bearings should almost always last longer than the wheels. Most bearing problems are caused by something getting into the bearings. In-line skates, skateboards, and scooters all have this problem. The reason you may not have had problems with your bike bearings is because the bearings are farther off the ground. With skates, skateboards, and scooters, the bearings are right down there close to the dirt.

Sand, mud, and gravel cause the most problems with scooter bearings. These are all things that you will find in the local playground or park, so it is not surprising that they get into scooter bearings. Even riding around near a sandbox can get sand in your bearings.

Scooting through water—especially muddy water—can hurt your bearings. After the water evaporates, whatever mud or dirt that was dissolved in it stays in the bearing casing.

Finally, keep the area around the wheels and forks clean. Any dirt that collects there can work its way into the bearings.

The bearings are the most sensitive part of the scooter. Take care of them and they will take care of you.

CHECK YOUR WHEELS AND BEARINGS REGULARLY EVEN IF YOU RIDE YOUR SCOOTER MOSTLY INDOORS. HAIR AND CARPET FIBERS CAN COLLECT IN THE SCOOTER'S AXLE AND WHEEL. THIS STUFF SHOULD BE CLEANED OUT REGULARLY BEFORE IT WORKS ITS WAY INTO THE BEARINGS.

Scooter Tip #7

NEVER ATTACH ANY ACCESSORY TO YOUR SCOOTER THAT REQUIRES YOU TO REMOVE A HAND FROM THE HANDLEBARS TO OPERATE. AND NEVER ATTACH AN ACCESSORY THAT IS SO HEAVY THAT IT RUINS THE BALANCE OF THE SCOOTER.

More is not better: Remember that cleaner is not always better. Just use as much as it says on the container. Using too much will not get your scooter any cleaner. And always read directions on the label for how to use any cleaner.

Shine it up: Use a soft cloth when polishing. A piece of worn-out clothing made out of cotton works best. Try not to get the cleaner all over the grip tape.

Deck Maintenance

Your deck is going to get dirty, so you should clean it regularly, using a mild soap and paper towels or a rag. A mild citrus-based cleaner is also good for decks.

Different kinds of decks require different kinds of care, so check the manual that came with your scooter to see what works best. If your deck is aluminum—for example, the Razor—you can use a mild metal polish wherever there isn't grip tape or stenciled printing. Metal polish can remove grip tape and paint. So be careful.

For jobs like getting out tar or even paint, use a citrus-based cleaner, nail polish remover, or something stronger. A very fine steel wool pad can be used on tough spots, but it may leave tiny scratches.

And remember to clean the bottom of the deck. That's where the dirt and grime really collect.

If your deck is wooden, check your local skateboard shop for products to use on wood decks.

BEAT-UP DECKS

Some decks crack or get chunks knocked off them. It doesn't happen often, but it does happen. With the Razor-type scooters, the deck is part of the frame, so you can't repair it.

Wood decks, on the other hand, can and will crack. Luckily, these decks are often designed so that they can be replaced. If your wood deck is cracked, replace it. Riding around on a scooter with a cracked deck can be dangerous.

Grip Tape Maintenance

Grip tape is that sand-papery tape on the scooter's deck. You must have grip tape on your scooter for a secure and safe ride. Grip tape is there for your protection. If for any reason it comes off, then replace it as soon as possible.

Some manufacturers offer replacement grip tape. Other manufacturers will not replace grip tape. There is a solution. Skateboard shops (and on-line Internet skateboard shops) sell a huge variety of stylish grip tape for decks. Even if you don't need new grip tape, it is a good way to customize your scooter.

Grip tape wears out, too. When it becomes worn and old, it should be replaced. You can tell if your grip tape needs replacing by the way it feels. If it is worn through so that you can see the deck in spots or if your foot slides around on the deck, then replace it.

REPLACING GRIP TAPE

If you scoot around a lot, then your grip tape will wear out. Sometimes it will peel up at the edges and come off completely.

Luckily, if your grip tape wears out or falls off, it can easily be replaced. Nearly every single skateboard shop and on-line skateboard supplier sells the stuff. Plus, it comes in a lot of colors, patterns, and roughness.

If you have a narrow-bodied scooter, be careful when buying grip tape with a pattern or picture. That's because most of the patterns are for wider, skateboard decks. In fact, some skateboarders have the entire deck of their boards covered with grip tape.

The first thing you have to do when replacing tape is to figure out how much you need. Basic grip tape is available in a long roll, but the store will sell you a piece that is the right size.

Start by making a pattern of your deck or the area you want to cover with tape. Place a large sheet of paper over the deck and trace the shape of the deck or the area you want to cover with tape on the paper. Next, carefully cut out the shape you just drew on the paper. (Get an adult to help you with this stuff if you aren't good at drawing or tracing.)

Now, take the pattern to the skate shop and buy a little more tape than you need. Once you have the grip tape, take your pattern and trace it around the edges on the smooth side of the tape. Then just cut the grip tape to size. Again, you may want to have an adult help you with this.

When you have your tape cut to the right size and style, peel off the back and attach it to the scooter's deck. Once you peel off the back of the tape, it's really, really sticky. You want to put it on the deck perfectly the first time, because it's very difficult to pull up and rearrange once it's down. Also, be sure that it's applied smoothly to the deck without creases or folds in it.

Steering Column and Handlebars

These should be wiped down with a mild citrus-based cleaner regularly. If you have a scooter that folds up, check all the joints and bolts. If you can turn them with your hand, then they are too loose. Tighten them up or have an adult tighten them.

Also check all of the locking mechanisms on the steering column. They shouldn't be cracked or worn or loose. While you are doing your inspection, unfold the scooter as if you are about to ride it and check for wiggle in the steering column. All of the locks should be firm, and all of the moving parts should move freely.

When a component such as a plastic locking mechanism breaks or cracks, don't try to fix it yourself with glue. Replace it. And if you misplace a part or it falls off when you are riding, then replace it with factory-authorized parts. You can get these replacement parts from a scooter dealer or directly from the manufacturer.

Remember: A loose bolt or a cracked locking mechanism—small problems—can, if not corrected, turn into big problems.

Your handlebar grips should also be in good shape. If they wear out, then replace them. Manufacturers and dealers sell replacement grips for scooters, but a lot of bike grips also fit scooters. Note: Before you buy bike grips, measure the handlebars' length and diameter to make sure they fit.

IMPORTANT: WHEN YOU REPLACE YOUR HANDLEBAR GRIPS, THEY SHOULD FIT SNUGLY TO THE BAR. IF YOU CAN PULL THEM OFF AT ALL, IT SHOULD BE VERY DIFFICULT. DON'T USE OIL OR ANYTHING THAT WON'T EVAPORATE TO EASE A NEW SET OF GRIPS ONTO THE HANDLEBARS. OIL WILL KEEP YOUR GRIPS LOOSE FOREVER, AND LOOSE GRIPS ARE DANGEROUS!

The Brake

The brake is one of the most important parts of your scooter. Whether you have a rear pressure brake controlled by your foot or a bike-style grip on the handlebars or some other type of brake setup, pay attention to how well it works and fix it at the first sign of trouble.

The brake on the Razor and other scooters like it is very simple. It's a rear pressure brake that you just push down on with your foot. The curved fender puts pressure on the wheel and slows or stops the scooter.

You should make sure that the brake system is kept clean of dirt and mud and sand. Clean out the little slot between the brake and the deck. If too much dirt gets stuck there, it can seriously hurt your braking power.

Also, inspect the spring to be certain that it is working correctly and not too loose.

Last, clean the underside of the brake itself. Mud and dirt on that underside isn't good for your stopping power.

If you have a braking system that works with a cable, like a hand brake on a bike, then adjust the cable and check all components as your would on your bike. After a while, these cables can stretch, reducing your braking power.

Cable and hand-brake type braking systems take a while to loosen up on new scooters. Avoid hills and racing until your brake works easily.

Scooter Tip #8

A PRETTY GOOD ANKLE GUARD CAN BE MADE FROM THE FOAM LINING OF A PAIR OF OLD IN-LINE SKATES. SIMPLY CUT OUT THE FOOT PORTION OF THE FOAM SO THAT THE LINING LOOKS LIKE A SOCK WITHOUT THE FOOT PART. THIS WORKS BEST WHEN THE FOAM COMES DOWN YOUR SHIN AND A LITTLE OVER YOUR SHOE. FOR BEST RESULTS, PUT THE FOAM ON YOUR FOOT AND TRACE WHERE YOU WANT TO CUT WITH CHALK. WARNING: ASK YOUR PARENTS BEFORE DOING THIS! BETTER YET, ASK THEM TO HELP YOU WITH THE CUTTING PART, WHICH CAN BE TRICKY.

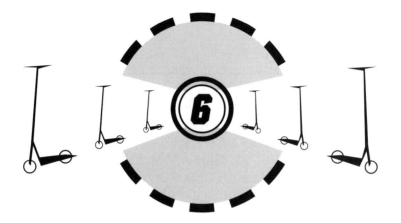

How and Where to
Buy Your Next Scooter

Chances are good that you already have a scooter. Maybe you want another scooter. Or maybe your first scooter broke and can't be fixed. Here are some guidelines for shopping:

Do the research. There are a lot of choices when it comes to scooters today, so take your time and shop around. Ask friends and relatives about the scooters they have. Compare prices between different stores. Go on-line to the different companies' Web sites and check out the options and features of each scooter. Learn as much as you can about the choices out there.

Buy right. Get the scooter that is right for you. If a deck is too big or too small, then don't buy that scooter. It should also be within your price range. Remember, the fanciest and most expensive scooter is not always the best one for you. Think about where you are going to ride it and how often. Talk over the different features and options with your parents.

Check out the store. There are more places than ever to buy scooters. You can buy one on-line, at a big mega-store, or at a small scooter and skate shop. If you buy at the mega-store, you might not be able to test-drive the scooter. Also, you may not find a salesperson there that knows about scooter features and repair.

Many small skateboard and in-line skate stores sell scooters, too. A good store may not offer the best price, but the salespeople should be able to answer any and all questions you may have. Plus, you can always return there if you have any repair problems or want to upgrade your bearings or handlebar grips. Usually, a smaller shop will allow you to test-drive the scooters. You may find a shop where the guys who run it are "too cool" to deal with scooters, kids, and a bunch of questions. If this is so, go someplace else. You're too cool to buy your scooter from them.

On-line shopping is pretty good if you know exactly what you want and are willing to wait for it. But even if you don't plan to buy your scooter on-line, it's still a great way to compare features and learn about the different scooters. The bad part is that you can't test-drive the scooters. Manufacturers' Web sites often list authorized dealers around the country. If you know what scooter you want, then you can look up a dealer near you and take it for a test drive.

Don't rush. Don't rush into buying the first scooter you see, whether it's on-line, in a large store, or in a small local store. Compare a variety of different scooters and stores.

Ask questions. Ask about the return policy and warranties. Nothing is worse than being stuck with a scooter that falls apart or can't be taken back if something breaks on it.

Watch out for counterfeits. There are a lot of counterfeit Razor scooters out there. If you see a scooter that says Razor on it but looks cheesy—for instance, it has the wrong type of wheels—stay away from it. Counterfeit scooters are poorly made from inferior parts.

Scooter Tip #9

DON'T ATTEMPT TO DO THE SAME KINDS OF TRICKS ON A SCOOTER THAT YOU DO ON YOUR BIKE, IN-LINE SKATES, OR SKATEBOARD. THE WHEELS AND BALANCE ARE ENTIRELY DIFFERENT. SCOOTERS ARE NOT DESIGNED FOR SUCH TRICKS.

Shopping Checklist

1. Make sure all the components don't wiggle, including wheels, brake, and handlebars. If you buy a folding-type scooter, the scooter should fold and unfold smoothly, and all the components should lock firmly into place.

2. Check the durometer rating on the wheels. If the wheels are too hard or soft, ask the clerk if the store can change them before you purchase the scooter. They may charge you extra, but at least you are getting the wheels you need. A scooter should have wheels with bearings! Some very cheap scooters don't have bearings—just axles in wheels, like little red wagons. These scooters will not last.

3. Make sure the wheels spin smoothly and evenly. Also, check the brake to make certain it works, and check out the steering to be sure it moves easily.

4. Inspect the edges of the grip tape to be certain it is tacked down all the way. A loose edge will only get worse with wear and tear.

5. If you are buying a wide-body scooter, with a deck of wood, fiberglass, or similar materials, check the deck for flex. Aluminum or metal decks generally don't have flex.

6. Check for steering column height. If the scooter has a steering column that doesn't adjust, it should be the perfect height. If the column is too tall or too short for comfortable scooting, then don't buy it.

7. Scooters should have no sharp edges anywhere on them.

Accessories

*T*here are a lot of accessories out there for your scooter. Some are made just for scooters and some are intended for bikes and skateboards but can be used for scooters.

These accessories can serve a real purpose or can be just for fun. However, whatever accessories you choose, they should be safe. Anything that gets in the way of safe scootering is a bad choice—no matter how cool it looks.

Water bottle holders. These are mostly made for bikes, but they can also be attached to scooters. If you have the type of scooter that folds up small, you might want to test some of the more compact holders to make sure they fit when your scooter is folded. If you get one of the larger styles, position it on the front of the steering column at about knee level. Remember, a water bottle holder should be attached to the part of the steering column that doesn't telescope into the lower part.

Bells. These are pretty cool. Bike bells can be attached to your scooter handlebars. Just be sure to locate the bell close enough to the hand grip so that you can easily reach it. Squeeze horns are fun on a bike, but shouldn't be tried on a scooter because you have to take your hand off the handlebars to work them. Bells are better because you work them with one finger.

Pouches and packs. You can easily mount a fanny pack or another type of small pack on the front of your handlebars. Some kids are even strapping their school backpacks onto the handlebars. But a backpack loaded with heavy books can unbalance the scooter and make riding dangerous. Even a heavy pack strapped to your back can throw your balance off.

Baskets. Small woven or metal baskets can also fit on scooter handlebars. These can be used for carrying stuff that isn't too heavy. However, if you overload the basket, it could be dangerous.

Lights. Bike lights on the handlebars and even helmet or clothing lights used for biking, skateboarding, and in-line skating are a good idea for safety reasons.

Handlebar Grips. Bike handlebar grips can also be used for scooters. Make sure you get the right size grip for a secure hold.

Custom grip tape. Skateboard shops sell many different styles of grip tape that can be used on scooters. Put a small strip of grip tape on the rear wheel brake on Razor-type scooters. This will help your heel grab the brake more firmly.

Custom handlebars: Safety should always be first in your mind when you begin replacing or changing important components on a scooter. However, in Japan, some kids began replacing the usual scooter handlebar with a BMX-style handlebar on their scooters. This is a major project and shouldn't be undertaken without adult supervision.

Wheelie bars. There are currently wheelie bars available for the Razor. These allow you to put your weight far back on the scooter to send the front end up in the air. These bars attach to either side of the wheel plate and come across the back in a kind of square U-shape.

Shock absorbers. Some scooters now come equipped with shock absorbers, such as the ones you find on BMX bikes. Do they work? Are they worth the extra money? Do you need them? Yes, they are working shock absorbers. They will smooth out some of the bumps for you and let you bounce the front end a little. Do you need them and are they worth the money? That is a different question. If you are riding on bumpy sidewalks, then they will make the ride a little smoother, but not that much.

THE OFFICIAL RAZOR WITH SHOCK ABSORBER LIMITS YOUR ABILITY TO REFIT YOUR SCOOTER WITH A LARGER WHEEL. LARGER WHEELS WON'T FIT ON THE SHOCK-ABSORBER MODEL.

Electronics. There is a lot of electronic gear available for bikes, including radios, lights, and even clocks. Choose any electronic gear carefully. Equipment that requires adjustment while riding is a bad idea because it means you have to take your hand off the handlebars. Also, scooters are sometimes just dropped on the ground. Thus a handlebar radio or light on a scooter is more likely to get broken than one on a bike.

When you are thinking of adding accessories, there are several things you should avoid:

1. Do not put anything on your scooter or attach anything to your scooter that adds a substantial amount of weight. Also, don't carry anything heavy in an attached basket or pack. Remember, balance is the key to safe scootering. An unbalanced load, whether it's attached to the scooter or just being carried in a basket, is unsafe.

2. Do not attach anything that sticks out in any direction beyond the span of your handlebars. This can be dangerous to people around you.

3. Do not attempt any major structural modifications to the scooter, like attaching a seat to it or changing the way the wheels fit into place.

4. Do not attach anything with a pointy tip or sharp edges to your scooter. This can not only be dangerous to you, but also to people around you.

Scooter Tip #11

CHECK OUT ALL HILLS. REMEMBER, HILLS THAT WERE EASY ON A BIKE CAN BE DANGEROUS TO GO DOWN ON A SCOOTER.

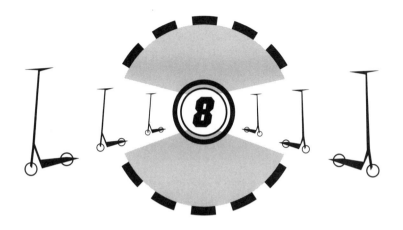

Tricks and Activities

All tricks and stunts can be dangerous. Ask any skateboarder. So if you don't feel comfortable doing them, then don't.

However, if you do choose to do tricks, stunts, or racing, take safety precautions. Wear appropriate safety gear and do them in a safe place, one not crowded with people walking or bike riding or in-line skating.

Trick Tip #1:

BUNNY HOPS, AIR HOPS, AND OTHER SCOOTER TRICKS ARE EASIER TO DO WHEN YOU ARE GOING SLOWER. JUST BECAUSE YOU ARE GOING FASTER DOESN'T MEAN YOU WILL HOP HIGHER. GO SLOW WHEN DOING TRICKS, ESPECIALLY IF YOU ARE JUST LEARNING THEM.

Bunny Hop

This is the simplest trick. The secret to a good bunny hop is the placement of your feet. Both feet should be securely on the deck and you should feel balanced. If your feet are not secure, you could slip off the deck. And if you do not have good balance, then you will land unevenly.

To try a bunny hop, get the scooter going slowly. Bending your knees a little, pull the scooter's handlebars up while jumping—not high, just a couple of inches to start. What you are actually doing is pulling the scooter's two wheels up off the ground as you take a small jump in the air. The deck should follow your feet up.

The main thing is to jump and pull the scooter by the handlebars up with you. If you do it right, you can't tell that you actually jumped with your feet. You are simply reducing the weight on the deck enough to pull the scooter up off the ground.

Good start: Firmly position yourself on the scooter. That means, get your best balance and stance. It usually helps to bend your knees a little, but not too much. Also, you should not be too far up front or too far towards the back of the scooter.

Pull: Holding the handlebars securely, pull hard...

And jump: If you pull and jump at the same time, the scooter should come up off the ground.

Perfect landing: There's no easy way to land softly with a Bunny Hop.

When you get good at bunny-hops, then you'll be able to hop over cracks and bumps in the sidewalk.

Try it going slowly at first. Then with a little bit of practice, you'll be able to bunny-hop at almost any speed.

Air Hop

This trick is very much like the bunny hop, but instead of keeping your feet on the scooter's deck, lift them off in midair. This will make it look like you're doing a skateboarder's Ollie. When you do this trick, you must have a good grip on the handlebars and your feet must be positioned in the center of the board.

Start easy: Start the Air Hop just like the Bunny Hop. Get your best balance on the scooter as close to the center as you can.

Pull up: Pull up on the handlebars like you do with a Bunny Hop.

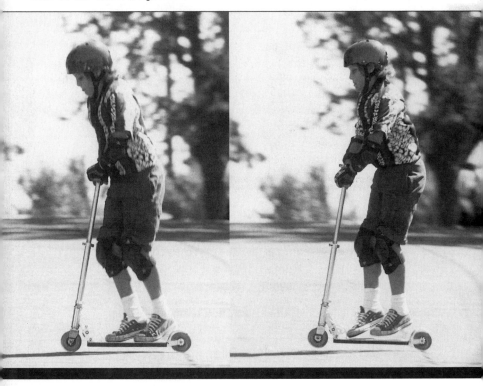

Jump up: Jump up just like you do with a Bunny Hop, only higher. If you time the jump right, the deck will still be a little below you as you jump. It's all in the timing and the height of your jump. This scooter trick takes a little practice.

Deck down first: If you jump carefully, then you should come down on the deck just after the deck comes down on the ground. Like all tricks, you should practice this going very slowly.

When you see somebody do the air hop, you see the board in the air, with the person's feet above the board.

Air hops can be done in three parts:

1. Jump up as with a bunny hop, pulling the scooter with you.

2. Let the scooter's deck fall away from your feet a little by bending your knees slightly.

3. Land on the scooter's deck.

Happy landings: Come down with both feet at once on the deck. The secret to a good landing is not to move your feet left or right when you are in the air, so that they remain over the deck the entire time you are in the air.

Wheelie

Everyone knows what a wheelie is on a bike: it's when you pull the front wheel up and ride on the back wheel for a while. You can do the same trick on a scooter, but it takes some practice.

Manufacturers are now selling wheelie bars for some scooters, particularly the Razor types. The wheelie is easy on a bike, but is harder on a scooter. The wheelie bar, which attaches to either side of the rear wheel plate, comes across the back to give you a little platform to stand on.

The secret of doing a wheelie is to shift most of your weight to the rear of the scooter while pulling up on the handlebars. By shifting your body weight to the back of the

Slow start: Start out slow with both feet as far back on the scooter as you can manage and still keep good balance.

Pull up: Pull up hard on the front. The best way to learn this trick—and all tricks—is to go slow. You don't have to be going fast to pop a scooter wheelie.

scooter, you can pull the front end up and do a wheelie. These wheelies don't last long, but it can be a fun trick.

Wheelies are more dangerous—that is to say, you are more likely to fall—than bunny hops.

If you are an in-line skater or skateboarder, you may be tempted to try some of the tricks and stunts you learned on your skates or board with your scooter. This can be very dangerous. Scooters can become extremely unsafe when you attempt tricks such as Ollies and grinding.

Up, up, up: Depending on how good your balance is, you can get a pretty high wheelie. But remember to stay at the back of the scooter.

Down, down, down: Let the scooter down as softly as you can. Hard landings for wheelies and hops are not good for bearings.

Scooter Tip #12

BE CAREFUL ON SLICK SURFACES, SUCH AS INDOOR FLOORS AND TILES. SURFACES THAT YOUR BIKE TIRES GRIP EASILY CAN BE MORE DANGEROUS ON A SCOOTER.

Trick Tip #2:

RAMPS AND JUMPS ARE A REALLY BAD IDEA FOR SCOOTERS AND YOU. FOR ONE THING, THEY CAN BE VERY HARSH ON YOUR SCOOTER'S BEARINGS, EVEN IF YOUR SCOOTER HAS SHOCK ABSORBERS. FOR ANOTHER THING, THEY ARE DANGEROUS. A JUMP THAT YOU'VE DONE A BILLION TIMES BEFORE ON YOUR SKATEBOARD CAN BE MUCH, MUCH MORE DANGEROUS ON YOUR SCOOTER.

Racing

You can choose to race against the clock or directly against your opponent or opponents. Whichever way you select, there are a few basic safety rules to follow.

Trick Tip #3:

IF YOU FEEL YOU'RE ABOUT TO FALL, THEN LET GO AND STEP OFF THE SCOOTER. BECAUSE THE WHEELS ARE SO SMALL AND CLOSE TO THE GROUND, IT WON'T GET BEAT UP BY THE FALL VERY BADLY. IT'S ALWAYS BETTER TO DROP THE SCOOTER THAN TO FALL YOURSELF.

OOPS! It's always better to "step off" a scooter if you lose your balance in mid-wheelie or hop. Just step off of the scooter if you start to fall.

Basic Racing Rules

◎ Never race down steep hills. The reason for this is simple: in the heat of competition, you may forget how fast you can go and exceed the limits of both your scooter and yourself.

◎ Never race where there are people walking, skating, or skateboarding.

◎ Never race toward a wall. It's hard to stop a scooter when it's racing toward a wall . . . Ouch!

◎ Always leave enough room on either side of you and your opponent. This may mean that sidewalk racing is out, too. Narrow sidewalks are not good racetracks for scooters.

◎ Never touch or bump your opponent while racing. This is not only bad sportsmanship but dangerous for you and your opponent.

◎ Be familiar with the track. When you are scooting around at cruising speed and hit a large crack or bump, it can eat your wheel. When you are racing and hit a bump or crack, it can send you flying to the ground.

Scooter Tip #13

THERE ARE THREE BASIC THINGS TO LOOK FOR IN A HELMET: STRAP STRENGTH; ROLL-OFF (DOES THE HELMET STAY IN PLACE DURING AN ACCIDENT?); AND IMPACT STRENGTH. CHECK CONSUMER PRODUCT SAFETY COMMISSION STANDARDS BEFORE BUYING A HELMET. ALSO, BUY A HELMET THAT YOU FIND IS COMFORTABLE. A HELMET THAT IS UNCOMFORTABLE TO WEAR WON'T GET WORN AND WON'T DO ANYONE ANY GOOD.

BEAT THE CLOCK

If the sidewalk or area where you want to race is too narrow for two scooters at once, here's another possibility. Instead of racing directly against your opponent, keep score by using a stopwatch. Many of the new digital wristwatches have this feature. Racing against time also reduces the chance of collisions with your opponent.

A slalom course of course: Two-liter soda bottles filled with water make a great slalom course. The object is to zigzag between the bottles without knocking them over. Ten bottles are a pretty challenging course for a driveway. It's important to set the bottles up in a straight line.

SODA BOTTLE SLALOM RACING

You have probably seen skiers do this in the Olympics. You set up a straight line of obstacles that you have to zigzag around, first on one side, then on the other.

Large plastic soda bottles filled with water make a great slalom course. To make the racecourse interesting, you will need between seven and ten bottles. Set them up in a straight line with lots of space between them. The closer the bottles are together—the shorter the distance between them—the harder the course is to complete.

Scooter racers lose points if they knock one of the bottles down, if they miss zigzagging between two bottles, or if they fall down.

DOWNHILL AND FLAT SLALOM

The two basic tracks you can set up for a slalom are downhill and flat surface. For the downhill slalom, the bottles should probably be set farther apart. Remember, the scooter is naturally gaining speed as it goes down a hill. For downhill racing you have to decide before the race whether the racers are allowed to push off once they start the course or if they have to glide all the way down the hill.

For flat surface racing, you can place the bottles closer together. And you have to decide whether the racers can push off once they begin the race or if they have to glide all the way through.

If you have a place where it can be done, it's fun to combine the flat and downhill slalom by using two sets of bottles. Set up one course on the hill and another course at the bottom of the hill on a flat surface.

To really make it a tough race, make the distance between the two sets of bottles different on the downhill and flat surface.

Whether you are racing downhill or on a flat surface it is always a good idea to have a starting line and a finish line. That way, it's easier to keep track of time if you use a stopwatch to see how fast someone finishes the course. Just start the stopwatch when the racer passes the starting line and stop it when the racer passes the finish line.

Here are several different possibilities for a slalom race.

◎ Set the bottles up on a slight incline and mark off a starting point. Racers can push themselves to the starting point, but then they have to have both feet on the deck. In this race, you lose points for pushing to gain speed once you pass the starting mark.

◎ Set the bottles up on a flat surface or a slight hill and just race for speed. After everyone has completed the course, move the bottles closer together and race again. Then move them even closer together. You'll be surprised at how difficult the race gets as the bottles are moved closer together.

◎ The circular slalom is really only good on a flat surface. Set the bottles up in a large circle or oval and race around them. You can set your own number of laps for the race.

◎ You can also do a "there and back" slalom course by setting up a straight line of bottles and racing from one end to the other and then back again.

POWER GLIDES

This isn't really a race, but it is lots of fun. Find a large open space and draw a starting line with chalk. Racers can then go behind the line and scoot up as fast as they can. However, once they pass the starting line, they aren't allowed to push again. This is really a distance competition to see how far they can scoot. You can do this either as a head-to-head competition or one at a time. Note: Only scooters with the same size wheels should compete against each other. Larger wheels have a real advantage.

Scooter Tip #14

SOFTER WHEELS DO GIVE A MORE COMFORTABLE RIDE, BUT ARE SLOWER AND MAY GET CHEWED UP BY SIDEWALKS MORE QUICKLY. IF YOU ARE RIDING YOUR SCOOTER ON A BUMPY, CRACK-FILLED SIDEWALK, YOU MAY WANT TO THINK TWICE ABOUT SOFTER WHEELS.

SCOOTER BOWLING

Set the ten plastic soda bottles you used for slalom racing like bowling pins. Draw a starting line with chalk. Taking turns, bowl yourself toward the plastic containers. You aren't allowed to push off once you pass the starting line, so the soda bottle pins should be far enough away to make hitting them interesting. Also, you aren't allowed to kick any of the pins down.

SCOOTER RELAY

This can be a really fun race, especially if you play it with adults. Set up a track in a park and have a regular relay race, but instead of handing off a baton or flag to the next runner, hand off the scooter to ride. This is a great game if you have a bunch of adults and kids, but only a few scooters. Plus, it's a goof watching the adults ride the scooters.

Gimme a Brake!

Scooter brakes are a lot different than brakes on your bike. They're great for slowing down, but not that good for quick stops. This can be dangerous when you get to a street corner and need to stop before crossing. It can also be dangerous when you go down hills. You may not be able to stop in time.

You can see this for yourself. Ride your bike at a comfortable speed and stop. Notice how long it takes to come to a full stop. Then go at the same speed on your scooter and stop. You'll see how many more feet of pavement it takes to stop a scooter than a bike.

That's why you should always plan ahead when you're riding your scooter. Start slowing down before you reach the corner. Also, when going down hills, use your brake to keep from building up too much speed. Remember, it's a lot easier to use the brake to keep from going too fast than to use it to slow down once you're going too fast.

There's also a pretty cool thing you can do to modify your brakes to make them safer. The standard rear-wheel-friction brakes are just made of plain metal. This looks pretty good, but if your foot or the metal gets wet, then it's really slippery. Even if it's not slippery, your foot can still slide off it.

To fix this, you'll need some good old-fashioned grip tape. Cut out a small strip and attach it to the brake where your foot goes. This will keep your foot from slipping. If you want to get fancy about it, then you can cut out small strips and make something like tiger stripes on the brake. Or you can cut out little circles and put them on the brake.

Which Is Faster, a Scooter or a Bike?

*I*f you said, "Bike, of course," then you weren't completely right. According to the folks that make Xootr, a scooter is faster for short trips up to three-fourths of a mile. Now, before you take bets against your biker friends, the Xootr folks probably didn't mean that a scooter is faster than a bike in a race. They were just talking about the time it takes to get somewhere riding normally.

You can argue about this with friends, but the fact remains, when you get to where you are headed on a bike, you still have to park it and lock it up. With a scooter, you don't lock it up, you just pick it up.

Scooters are a lot of fun. But just as with a bike or in-line skates, you have to follow the rules of the road even if you only scoot around on the sidewalk and in parks.

Many kids aren't 100 percent aware of what they can and what they cannot do safely on a scooter. While scooters are similar in some ways to in-line skates, skateboards, and even bikes, they are different in other ways. This book should have made you aware of these similarities and differences.

Safety should always come first when you take your scooter out for a ride. That means being concerned not only for your own safety but also for the safety of the kids, pets, and adults around you.

The first rule of safety is knowing what your scooter can and can't do. The second rule is knowing what you can and can't do on your scooter. Get a sense of how fast you can safely go. Get to know how long it takes you to stop before reaching traffic. And understand that scooters were not intended to be high-speed vehicles.

Use your common sense! That's the third rule of safety.

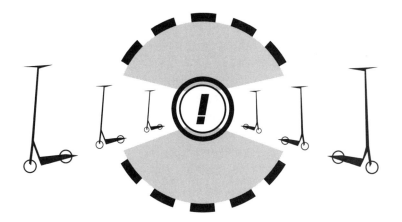

Glossary

Glossary

ABEC: This is short for Annular Bearing Engineering Committee. You might see the letters ABEC on your wheels and bearing case. The figure there tells you how precise the bearings are in the wheel. The higher the ABEC number—they go up to 9—the more precise the bearings. Many in-line skaters and skateboarders believe that the higher the ABEC number, the faster the bearings.

Allen Wrench: A wrench that works a lot like a screw-driver. It's also called a hex wrench. It has six sides and inserts into the hole at the center of the wheel. Many of the Razor-type scooters use a 5 mm Allen wrench. For best results, you should use two of these wrenches, one on either side of the wheel, to tighten and remove wheels.

Bearings: The circular wheel inside your wheel. The bearings contain metal balls that allow the wheel to spin freely around the axle.

Bunny Hop: A basic scooter trick in which both wheels of the scooter leave—along with the rider—the ground for a short distance.

Core: The hard center of your wheel. Also called a hub. The core is made out of rigid material that holds the bearings in place and keeps the wheel straight. There are two basic kinds of hubs: open core, in which you can see the spokes, and closed core, in which the spokes are hidden.

Deck: The part of the scooter you stand on. Decks can be made out of many different materials, including aluminum, wood, or carbon fiber. Some decks can be changed or replaced and other decks are attached to the scooter's frame.

Durometer: A device for measuring a wheel's softness and hardness. The higher the number, the harder the wheel.

Grip Tape: A self-adhesive tape that attaches to the scooter deck. The top side of grip tape is rough to the touch, like sandpaper. It provides a solid footing on the deck. Originally used for skateboards, grip tape is a scooter essential. It keeps your foot secure on the deck while you are scooting.

Hop-up Kits: A pre-packaged kit that includes frame spacers, bearing spacers, and axles. These let you tighten the wheels into place without ruining the spacers or hubs; they are most often used in the in-line skating world.

Hub: *See* Core.

Lube: Short for lubricant, which is a type of grease or oil used to keep the bearings moving smoothly.

Road Rash: A slang expression meaning a bad scrape from falling off your scooter, skateboard, or in-line skates.

Urethane: A petroleum-based plastic that many of today's Razor-type scooter wheels are made out of. In-line skates and skateboards also use urethane wheels. Urethane wheels are very durable and may be brightly colored.